Also by Robert Finch

Common Ground

The Primal Place

For Winifred —
Passionate defender of
the Narrow Land —
Best wishes,
Robert Finch

Craigville, August 18–24, 1996

The Primal Place

by Robert Finch

W · W · NORTON & COMPANY · NEW YORK · LONDON

Conrad Aiken's letter to Mary Aiken is reproduced by permission of The Huntington Library, San Marino, California.

"Mayflower" is from *Collected Poems* by Conrad Aiken, copyright © 1953, 1970 by Conrad Aiken; renewed 1981 by Mary Aiken. Reprinted by permission of Oxford University Press, Inc.

The text of this book is composed in V.I.P. Janson, with display type set in Caslon Openface & Thompson Quillscript. Composition and manufacturing by The Maple-Vail Book Manufacturing Group. Book design by Antonina Krass. Interior illustration by Peter Canfield Peck.

First Edition

Library of Congress Cataloging in Publication Data

Finch, Robert, 1943–
The primal place.

1. Natural history—Massachusetts—Cape Cod.
2. Cape Cod (Mass.) I. Title
QH105.M4F57   1983   574.9744′92   82–22566

ISBN 0-393-01623-4

W. W. Norton & Company, Inc., 500 Fifth Avenue, New York, N.Y. 10110
W. W. Norton & Company Ltd., 37 Great Russell Street, London WC1B 3NU

1 2 3 4 5 6 7 8 9 0

This book is for Beth,
Christopher, and Katy,
and for all Punkhorners,
past and present.

I feel like Ulysses. And so I fare west. Brewster begins to seem more than ever like the Primal Place—We shall see!
—CONRAD AIKEN

I only went out for a walk and finally concluded to stay out till sundown, for going out, I found, was really going in.
—JOHN MUIR

Contents

Digging In

CHAPTER 1

Into the Maze

1

One of the occupational hazards of living in a place like Cape Cod is not always knowing where you are. The sea fog that rolls in regularly over the mud flats and salt marshes is not entirely to blame for such chronic disorientation. Nor are the winter northeasterlies whose heavy surf and storm surges break through barrier beaches, destroy parking lots, silt up harbors, and claim waterfront property all that dislocate us.

Change is the coin of this sandy realm, and as long as we are not too close to it, such change delights us. The seasons flow in their rhythmic variety, a little out of sync with the mainland due to the ocean's moderating influence—which pleases our sense of separateness. With them come in the streaming tides of shorebirds, migrating alewives and striped bass, pack ice in Cape Cod Bay, spring peepers in the bogs, gypsy moths in the oaks, and tourists in the motels and restaurants.

Years flow and bring still broader changes, sometimes surprising, not always welcome. Bald heaths grow up to pine barrens, meadows fill in with juniper, abandoned bogs return to cedar swamps or maple swamps, oaks replace the pines, and a charming water view from the deck or terrace disappears under a rising horizon of leaves.

With these changes some new bird species appear, others grow scarcer. Fish populations fluctuate, ponds slowly silt in. New areas of tidal flats are claimed by spreading salt-marsh grasses, and each year a few more feet of the ocean cliffs topple into the surf, taking a beach cottage or two with them. Major alterations in the shape of the coastline can and do take place within a man's lifetime, adding a feeling of shared mortality in our relationship with this thin spar of glacial leavings. Yet through all this variety of natural change we also sense a continuity, not always to our liking, perhaps, but with a fittingness and perceptible identity of its own, an interplay of great and connected forces.

To this natural change, however, we have added our own, in a way that we share with most other parts of the country. In the beginning we may have desired only to "fit in" to this natural scene, to enjoy what it has to offer; and yet in doing so on such a mass scale and on our own terms, we have inevitably introduced forces that have had increasing repercussions of their own.

We move here in winter onto some quiet street and find the following summer that traffic makes it unsafe to cross the road for our mail. A piece of woods where we used to walk our dogs is turned, almost overnight, into roads and building lots. An open stretch of coastal bluffs that once formed a background to our clamming on the mud flats is now clotted with condominiums. Along the Mid-Cape Highway the deer we noticed for years are one day no longer there; in their stead are houses and tennis courts. Back roads and open fields, where fox stalked and woodcock courted, all at once sprout shopping malls, golf courses, new schools, and sewage-treatment plants. And so on.

Countryside is suddenly suburban, suburban areas become densely developed, and in places our highways and urbanized areas begin to take on an aspect that makes us look hard at the exit and street signs in order to reassure ourselves we are not in Boston or New Bedford, yet. Having increased our individual mobility in both the physical and social sense—the speed and ease with which we can travel from place to place as well as the power to choose our hometowns—we find ourselves less and less sure of where it is we have finally arrived.

Sometimes, watching a chickadee or a junco at the window feeder at the end of a winter's day, ruffled and tossed by a wet wind and alone at the coming of darkness, I am tempted to pity its lack of human comforts and security. But the bird at least was born to the condition in which it lives. It is part of an unbroken past of this land and knows where to find itself, despite all human and natural change, during the night and in the morning. Can I say as much for myself?

What is Cape Cod today? Rural? Semirural? Suburban? Seasonally urban? Bits and parts of each, perhaps. For this particular moment, at least, the term *subrural* seems as accurate as any: a patchwork of conflicting claims and uses hanging on to the remnants of a distinct rural culture that now exists almost completely in the past. And once we have named it, what then? What are we to make of it? How are we to know where we are? How are we to get here, once we have arrived?

2
_____

The first step must be to see clearly what is there. This is often more difficult than it might appear, for nature has no guile, which is one of the things that makes it so hard for us to see. The bare, uncompromising face of the land is too much for us to behold, and so we clothe it in myth, sentiment, and imposed expectations.

In West Brewster, for instance, where I live, the scene outside my window looks more like western Connecticut or Minnesota than like what most people think of as a typical Cape Cod landscape. No sandy shores or low dunes, no salt marshes or wide ocean waters stretch out before me. Rather, the house I built here a few years ago sits well inland, tucked into the wooded, hilly terrain of a low, broken line of glacial hills known as the Sandwich Moraine. The moraine begins west at the Cape Cod Canal, rises quickly to a height of just over 300 feet, runs east along the edge of Cape Cod Bay for some forty miles in a descending and increasingly interrupted ridge of loose till and rocks, and eventually peters out into the Atlantic at Orleans, where the arm of the Cape bends north toward Provincetown.

My house is situated near the eastern end of this moraine, on one of the lower crests about eighty feet above mean sea level. It faces south, on the north side of a roughly circular ridge of hills. These hills enclose a steep-sided bowl, or kettle hole, about a quarter of a mile in diameter, known locally as Berry's Hole.

The house is also circular in shape—octagonal, to be exact—with wide overhangs that combine with the higher hills around it to effectively block out most of the sky from inside, even in winter. When it was built, the top of the hill was leveled off and lowered a few feet, so that the yard, which stretches south from the house to the edge of the kettle hole, appears to leap off into nothing, into some great abyss, rather than falling off, as it does, into the rather modest hollow below.

The soil in these hills is sandy by mainland standards, but compared with beach sand it is heavy with clay and studded not only with small stones but also with many large glacial boulders twenty feet or more in length, called glacial erratics. Likewise, there is little of the low seaside vegetation generally associated with a shoreline environment—beach plum, bayberry, pitch pine. Instead, the surrounding slopes are covered with nearly pure stands of oak, that inland tree. For as far as I can see, unbroken stands of black and white oak lift their gray, lichen-spotted trunks and branches crookedly skyward.

Since the soil is relatively poor in nutrients, the oaks tend to be dwarfed in stature and prone to insect infestations. Nevertheless, they combine with the land to create an illusion of size. Stunted and twisted by poor soil, overcutting, and salt-laden winds, these trees possess the crooked look of age. They do not dominate the low hills but fit in proportion to them, so that together they give the impression of a far greater scale than either really has. It is easy to look out at them and see full-sized forests lining the flanks of mountain ranges that stretch for miles across some formidable gorge. The Cape has its own scale, and, to one not used to it, its landscape is full of such tricks of proportion and perspective.

No shorebirds, terns, herons, or crabs inhabit the immediate area. Rather, my wild neighbors are woodland fauna—deer, crows, owls, grouse, and a fox who lives in a burrow halfway down the hollow. Wood thrushes and phoebes nest about the house in summer, whippoorwills sing at night, and red-tailed hawks wheel slowly overhead, sending down sibilant screams from a high October sky. In the spring the slopes of Berry's Hole are covered with star flowers, lady's-slipper orchids, and trailing arbutus, or mayflower, while out of its deep, wet throat comes the tumultuous, insistent, nighttime chorus of wood frogs and spring peepers.

In short, although my home, as the herring gull flies, is less than half a mile inland from the salt marshes and shallow waters of Cape Cod Bay, it often takes an effort of will to remind myself that I live, not deep in the heart of the continent, but on an exposed and vulnerable headland thirty miles out into the open Atlantic, on the thin shores of a narrow land.

3

One May morning, several months after moving into the house, I looked up from the table where I had been typing and saw the stiff, gray, intersecting patterns of the oak trunks and branches outside the window. I saw them, as though for the first time, for what they really were: a maze, a vast, living maze stretching out beyond my lines of sight. And all at once I knew, with a clear and compelling conviction, that what I wanted, what I was seeking here, was entrance, or rather re-entrance, into that maze.

The trees are not an impenetrable thicket. They are, in fact, more like the original Cape Cod forest encountered by the Puritans during the *Mayflower*'s initial landfall at Provincetown in November of 1620 and described by Gov. William Bradford as "open and fit to go riding in." I can easily get up from my chair, open the door, cross the yard, and walk down the wooded slope to the bottom of the kettle hole. I have done so many times, before and since, but whenever I do my every noise and movement reveals me as an outsider, an intruder. I jangle my credentials as I go, crashing through the dry leaves, cursing as my jacket or pants leg catches on a barbed strand of catbrier.

What I want is to go silently and smoothly into the maze, without a rustle, as the light fox bounds with inborn agility across the rounded stone walls; as the soft rabbit threads itself surely and painlessly through the brier and viburnum jungles; as the lean, long-legged deer stops to look at me, sideways, with wet black eyes, then steps cleanly and quickly over brush and branch, disappearing up the slope without a word, as though into a fog; as the sharp-shinned hawk flits batlike through the web of branches; as the flicker leaps up and glides out through the layered oak boughs; as the green-and-gold garter snake, warming itself on a stone in the spring sun, suddenly bolts at my presence and, like a sand eel, vanishes in a glistening wriggle down into a crease in the earth and is gone.

These creatures tease me with their unconscious competence, a sureness that implies not so much prowess as belonging, of knowing where and who they are, of being local inhabitants in a way I am not.

Sometimes, frustrated by the unyielding rigidity of these woods in the face of my overtures, I go out with my chainsaw and cut down a few more of the trees around the house, pretending that I am getting firewood. For a few minutes the air is full of a geared thunder that obliterates all perception or participation, until the rashness of my deed catches up with me and I stop, finding myself in a space suddenly cleared and empty, surrounded by a quailed silence, having solved nothing and gotten nowhere.

There is no Gordian knot to cut here. Every part of the maze is a knot tied to every other part. To cut down the trees and scatter the animals, to make broad paths and wide clearings, is not to solve or enter the mystery, but to obliterate it and erect empty designs in its place. Such acts may give me passage and room to move about, but not entrance, and entrance is what I crave.

There is no quick, easy way into this or any other place, no sign pointing out the beginning of the path—no path to point out, for that matter. And yet, as I look out from this house into the round yard bordered by a sea of trees, and beyond them to the unseen shape of the peninsula itself, uncurling like a tendril growing into the sea, I seem to sense that this spot is as good as any from which to begin.

I take the sheet of paper, half-filled with sentences, out of the typewriter and hold it up before my eyes. Turning the sheet sideways, I look over its edge out the window to the trees beyond. When I do, the vertical lines of black ink begin to blur into the dark, rising bars of the trunks. It is a self-conscious gesture, but perhaps that is what it takes—a deliberate change of perspective, a loosening of focus, and a bending of your lines of sight to what it is you would see.

Or perhaps the secret is even simpler, as simple as the insistent, hidden song of the ovenbird, deep in the layered woods around me, that now begins to rise up out of the kettle hole in a ringing and ever more confident crescendo: *teach-er*, *Teach-er*, *TEACH-ER*, ***TEACH-ER!***

CHAPTER 2

Through the Glass Doors

1
___

So much in this world depends on where you sit down at the table. Ours, for example, stands in front of a series of large thermopane windows and sliding glass doors that fill the angled south walls of the house. The idea was to let in, under the wide overhangs, as much winter sun as possible, as well as to take advantage of the broad view out across the wooded slopes of the kettle hole beyond the yard.

Through these generous openings, sealed in winter, screened in summer, I watch the changing fashions of the seasons: the leaves falling, the grass growing, the birds coming and going, the transient Cape snows limning the bare oak branches. Sometimes I feel like Rod Taylor, in that marvelous time-lapse sequence from *The Time Machine* in which the hero, in evening clothes, sits in his stationary, elaborately Victorian machine, complete with red-plush chair and brass fittings, and watches with bemusement as the ever-accelerating tides of fashion and war pass before his eyes.

From time to time I witness little dramas, some repeated regularly, such as the murder of crows that raucously mob our resident great horned owl, harrying it relentlessly at all seasons round and round the perimeter of the wide bowl of Berry's Hole. Other episodes seem more like half-translated bits of life, barely glimpsed before they are gone. One winter morning I sat in my bathrobe at the table, comfortably eating breakfast next to the wood stove, while a hard wind shook the gray maze of trees outside and a cold rain dripped off the overhangs. There came a sudden flapping of brown and white down on the eastern flank of the kettle hole, where my neighbor's drive winds up the hill. At first it looked like a large paper bag or a sheet of newspaper blowing up the driveway, but then the branches parted in the wind and revealed a red-tailed hawk that had apparently just pounced on some mouse or small bird. A moment later the trees obscured it again, but the hawk stayed down there on the road, flapping wildly for several seconds, so that I thought it might be hurt. Then it pounced again, leaping several feet ahead, and banked grandly off down into the hole, carrying something limp and dark in its talons. Landing on some branch, it closed its wings and disappeared into the gloom of the day. Rain continued to drip off the eaves in a thin, tattered curtain. Death and drama over toast and tea.

Another morning, following a night's snowfall in January, I raised the shades before the glass doors and looked out onto a confectioner's delight, an intricate sugar fretwork of branches and twigs, a frozen tangle of snow wind through the woods. Across the yard and onto this whitened scene there swept a dark brown hawk with bent, pointed wings. It landed on a dead branch of a young black oak just at the edge of the yard, where I observed it imperfectly through sleet-spotted windows. It was a handsome bird, with a heavily streaked breast, distinctly barred tail, and a white eye stripe—a female pigeon hawk, or merlin. Rarely found on the Cape in winter, pigeon hawks are usually seen in open country or near the beach. This one was obviously in passage, but she stayed on the dead branch for several minutes, preening herself, spreading out her richly colored tail and wings, scratching her head with one leg like a dog, then, catlike, stretching out each leg and claw separately, shaking them as though to fluff up her feather leggings. Finally satisfied, she flew off to the west—a handsome apparition, richly brown and smooth in motion on pointed wings across a white landscape. I felt privileged to have caught her unawares, at toilette, for a few minutes. How many of us are that dignified and composed in our private moments?

2

I suppose I would see a great many more birds in winter from inside if I maintained a regular feeding program, but I prefer to keep things haphazard and take what comes. It is not only a matter of my not wanting the birds to become dependent on me, and of knowing they don't need to be. Having visited zoos, I also know I am not likely to get many insights into natural bird behavior at a feeding station. But even more, rather than attracting them to me, I want to be attracted to them, to let them win my confidence and coax me out of my hiding places at all seasons and hours, to see what treats or sustenance they might have to offer. Perhaps, like the tufted titmouse, which first arrived on Cape Cod only a generation ago, I too might find myself extending my range.

Nonetheless I sporadically hang out suet, fill up a single window feeder, and scatter grain and bread crumbs in the yard. I do it more for myself than for the birds; it helps me through the winter to have those bright bits of life, those hot, fluffy little balls of undiminished vitality jumping, pecking, preening, and flitting about in a world gone dead and barren.

Shortly after New Year's, I was again seated at the table, this time having lunch, when a large, iridescent blue jay alighted on the withered lawn outside and began feeding on some cracked corn I had spread out that morning. It would peck and look up, peck and look about, peck and turn, in continuous fashion. This jay, generally regarded as an aggressive and predatory bird, was yet ever watchful. It did not seem to eat to taste. It had no leisure to taste, had in fact no "meal" at all in the sense I did, but only another risky task to perform, and was bent solely on storing as much energy as it could as quickly and cautiously as possible.

The blue jay has few natural enemies, though I have seen it hide when a sharp-shinned hawk shows up, and have on occasion found jay feet in dissected owl pellets. But it is perpetually on guard and alert to danger, always tensed and ready to move quickly. It must forever eat and run, and that, it suddenly seemed, was the main difference between us. In my heated house, casually munching my prepared lunch, I have the luxury of watching this bird out of pure curiosity, to speculate on its nature or significance.

How quickly we lose sight of the complex artifices required to enable us to enjoy the simplest of human activities: eating a sandwich while watching a bird. Only yesterday, in the history of my race, I might have regarded the jay differently: as an unwelcome crier of my presence to local game, or perhaps as a morsel of food itself. More than in testing our physical fitness and aesthetic capacities on mountain peaks and along miles of trackless woods, the true wilderness experience may lie in our ability to see every other creature as a potential competitor or prey.

There is a covey of bobwhite quail in the neighborhood that regularly comes into the yard to feed in winter. This year there are eighteen, ten males and eight females, the males being readily distinguished by their sharp black-and-white face markings. Occasionally I see their heads peering up cautiously over the low stone wall that rims the back edge of the yard. If all is clear, they spill over onto the lawn all at once, like trench soldiers going up and over. But normally they appear singly, coming out between two stumps near the woodpile, as though down the ramp of a chicken house. They look, in fact, very much like chickens, scurrying with upstretched necks in a precipitous, forward-leaning manner across the yard. They dash one by one across the yard and form a line, pecking and bobbing their way along. For a few minutes my backyard becomes a barnyard, and I enjoy the pleasures of a poultry farm without any expense or benefit of zoning permits. Quail, I've been told, will at times actually feed with chickens in winter.

When I have put out corn for them they will spend most of their time with it, but they come even when there is none. I have watched them perambulate in a line completely around the house, eating grass blades. They do this not by pulling them up but by nipping each blade down to its root with two or three quick jabs, in the manner of rabbits. A covey of quail might conceivably prove useful in keeping a summer lawn trimmed, but bobwhite become secretive during hot weather when wild food is abundant.

If undisturbed, they will leave the yard as they arrived, quietly and on the ground. They slip off again, one by one, usually a male first, followed several seconds later by another, then another, and another—to gather again, uttering their querulous rally calls, somewhere in the hollow down below the house.

Their arrival and departure motion is curiously organic. It reminds me of an amoeba, first sending out a pseudopod and then flowing into it, a rhythmic extension and regrouping. Whether they leave in the exact order in which they arrive (which might indicate some strict pecking order) is something I haven't been able to determine. But a definite threadlike psychological connection running through the covey suggests the existence of a tight, if seasonal, group structure, like that of shorebird flocks. I have even seen them along the shoreline here, feeding with sanderlings and sandpipers among eelgrass thrown up by the tide.

By late spring the winter coveys begin to break up, as the quail pair off and disappear into the deeper woods to raise their broods. I do not expect to see them here again in front of the doors until late summer. The green wall begins to rebuild itself. By the first week in May the small grove of young beech trees on the slope beyond the yard have begun to unfurl their long, spiraled leaf buds, and soon the pale, thin, supple new leaves ripple all day long in the slightest breeze, like some green brook flowing horizontally below the house.

Just about this time we begin leaving the shades up after dinner, and the emerging beech leaves make a pattern of ornate lace against the evening skies. One evening, at the end of the meal, my wife, Beth, looked out the glass doors and said, "There's something very large in that tree out there."

I turned and looked, thinking it was probably a squirrel, but there, in the very top of one of the beeches, was the large, rounded shape of a ruffed grouse, feeding on the young leaf clusters. It gave me the same odd sensation that I had felt the first time I saw wood ducks or great blue herons sitting in trees, though I knew they all had good reasons for being there. But the grouse somehow looked even stranger, perhaps because of its comical, chickenlike silhouette and the apparent inadequacy of the thin branches to support its weight. A moderate breeze swayed and sprung the slender beech limbs so that the bird spent as much time maintaining or regaining its balance as it did stretching out its neck to pluck off more buds and leaves.

After a few minutes another grouse, which had apparently been feeding in the lower branches, fluttered up to join the first in the crown, and shortly thereafter two more joined them. Ruffed grouse are normally solitary birds, and four was more than I had ever seen together at one time.

The next day it rained, but the following evening another bird, quite likely one of the original quartet, appeared again in the top of the same beech, accompanied this time by a gray squirrel, which was also feeding on the budding leaves. The evening was clear and the wind even gustier then before. The squirrel, more daring than the grouse, fed further out at the very ends of the branches and lost its footing more than once, falling several feet through the branches before recovering itself.

The grouse, on the other hand, stayed close to the trunk on a main limb during the gusts, timing its forays out onto the branch to moments when the wind slackened. Despite the grouse's larger size and inferior tree-climbing ability, it had a better time of it as a whole than did the squirrel, which gave up after ten minutes or so and left.

The grouse stayed on, venturing out and retreating in counterpoint with the gusts and lulls, while the dying light, burning up through the crown of the tree, burnished the twigs and leaf buds. I pulled up a chair before the glass doors and sat down; through my binoculars I could still manage to get a good look at the bird and its colors as it huddled next to the trunk. The tail was a deep gray, but the head and neck were distinctly reddish brown, like the colors of a thrush's back, and its eyes gave that wide-eyed stare common to all gallinaceous birds. The neck was heavily streaked, though the black ruff was not visible.

Though the bird was only slightly above eye level from my perspective, it must have been a good twenty-five feet off the ground, balancing itself in gusts exceeding twenty knots. My initial surprise and amusement now gave way to a rush of admiration for the unexpected grace and expertise of this ground-dwelling bird. When it fed, I could see that it carefully plucked the green embryonic leaves out of their cases, leaving the pale copper papery shells attached to the twigs.

I sat there watching the bird feed for a long time, until I was no longer watching anything but a blank screen gone dark. Just then my family, having gone out after dinner for some ice cream, returned and found me sitting in a chair before glass doors staring through a pair of field glasses into the night. I must have looked at least as absurd to them as the grouse feeding in the top of a tree had at first looked to me, and their comments were kinder than they might have been.

But it seems now that the importance of the experience had something to do with watching a creature utterly wild in a position of unaccustomed exposure. Because the situation was new and unexpected, it was also remarkably free of any limiting preconceptions on my part. At any given moment, I had no idea what might happen next. The whole episode was as new and as old as the first dawn and seemed to lay upon me an obligation to witness, observe, and fix the texture of it in my mind as long and as faithfully as I could.

About a week after the beeches leaf out, the oaks follow, bubbling over with fountains of beaded catkins and small, arched, downy leaves that glisten with dew and thicken in the trees each day like a slow, pink fog.

During the first part of May, I am likely to catch a glimpse of the Cape's rather thin and unpredictable stream of spring warblers. On occasion, in their rush northward, sizable waves of these birds will spill out among the tasseled oaks for half an hour or so—dozens of black-and-whites, parulas, Blackburnians, magnolias, blackpolls, and Tennessees, like tiny jewels flitting from branch to branch, giving off high buzzy trills and thin whistles as they search for early insects and grubs among the still-embryonic leaves—before blowing away again on the next breeze.

The warblers are followed quickly by the May flood of returning breeding birds: kingbirds, great crested flycatchers, phoebes, vireos, ovenbirds, wood thrushes, catbirds, towhees, and occasionally a brilliant tanager or two. Their arrival is timed to coincide roughly with the emergence of the new insect crop on which they will raise their new broods. But it seems also designed to frustrate my eye, which usually manages to catch just a few clear glimpses of these birds before the lime and pink haze of the new leaves solidifies into the solid green wall of summer. Whatever domestic dramas take place in their branches from June to September play themselves out for the most part behind this opaque curtain.

But energy levels are still high in early summer, and June bursts through in noise and color. Bright orioles posture in the treetops like orange fruit, dripping song all day long. Flickers and blue jays hold curious conventions in the lower branches. The flickers usually appear in pairs, or trios, going at one another nonstop with their insistent, whiplike calls. The jays gather in groups of half a dozen or more, bowing deeply and politely to one another as they exchange their rusty "pump-handle calls."

On the new summer grass the robins alight, characteristi-cally cocking their heads to one side, as though listening for the worms they seek underground. When the weather finally turns dry, with the first long hot spell, small flocks of cowbirds are likely to show up, taking the place of the winter quail to peck in the grass. These drab, dour-looking, brown-headed blackbirds always conjure up a medieval scene in my mind. With muffled walk and downcast eyes, they move along like hooded monks, humbly and industriously gleaning in the grainfields. The fact that the cowbirds actually lead parasitic, promiscuous lives, depositing their eggs in the nests of other birds and leaving the chicks to be raised by foster parents, only adds an ironic edge to the fancy.

Suddenly, among their number, a handsome gray prince descends, chevrons flashing, to survey his lands. The regal mockingbird (himself sometimes a victim of these cowbirds) sings cosmopolitan and merry as he watches the holy cacklers from the lofty height of a nearby blueberry bush. Knight and horse in one, he stops nowhere for long but constantly darts and flits everywhere with energy and good feeling, a good-natured reproach to the humorless industry of the bird monks. I put my hand against the glass, and the scene instantly dissolves, the birds fleeing like dismissed players into the woods.

By late June most of the birds have become secretive, quietly busy at the vital task of raising young. The jays mysteriously disappear into deeper woods. Songs cease, shriveling in the heat of July, except for the indefatigable wood thrushes, pewees, and red-eyed vireos, who prolong their daylong songs well into the dog days of August. Apart from the ubiquitous mourning doves and the always-sociable chickadees, the stage beyond the glass doors is usually bare for most of the day in midsummer.

3

One day in July, during a prolonged spell of hot, dry weather, I noticed that a small patch of grass directly in front of the glass doors had taken on a strange, lumpy appearance, bulging slightly above the surrounding ground, as though it were a bowl of bread dough that had begun to rise in the summer heat. I went outside to investigate and stepped into the middle of a violent war.

It was an ant battle, and apparently one of no mean proportions. An area of several square yards was thickly covered with thousands of ants scurrying about in seemingly random motion. They were mostly red ants, with blackish abdomens, about three-eighths of an inch long. Taking a closer look, I saw that a smaller number of larger black ants were engaged in battle with some of the reds. Most of the red ants, however, were emerging from small granular mounds built between the grass tufts and were carrying white naked larvae, nearly as large as themselves, in their mandibles.

The "war" covered quite a large area and extended, in places, halfway across the yard. For several minutes I stood entranced,

trying to impose some pattern of purpose on the insects' frantic, serrated motions. Knowing very little about ants, I assumed
that the red-ant colony had been invaded by a foray party of
blacks that had gotten down into the subterranean nurseries,
creating panic and sending the reds into a massive rescue effort
to remove their larvae to safety.

Two aspects of the battle, however, threw some doubts on
my impromptu analysis. First, for invaders, the black, seemed
strangely nonaggressive. There were no pitched fights to the
death here. For the most part there were only brief harrying
maneuvers by the reds, as two or three ganged up on a black
for a minute or so and then let go and rushed off. Also, I saw
no attempts by the blacks to take away the larvae from the
reds. Perhaps, I began to think, the black ants had stumbled
upon the reds' nests by mistake and were trying to extricate
themselves.

But there was another curious thing. Although the red ants'
movements at first seemed random, I noticed after a time that
the larvae-carrying ants were actually retreating in a definite
direction in loose columns forming a swath five to six feet wide.
I followed this swath southwesterly across the yard for about
thirty-five feet (roughly the equivalent of a mile to these tiny
creatures) and eventually saw the red ants disappearing with
their white-larvae burdens into other ant mounds near our
strawberry patch.

At this point, my theories in shambles, I myself made a judi-
cious retreat to the nearby Cape Cod Museum of Natural History, where I work, to seek some factual reinforcement. In the
museum's library I found no dearth of literature on ants; myr-
mecologists, it would seem, are a prolific lot. After leafing
through a dozen or so books on the subject for nearly an hour,
I began to construct a more scientific, or at least more plausi-
ble, explanation of the morning's events, which was nonetheless a good deal stranger than my own ignorant fictions. Warfare
among ants is indeed a widespread phenomenon and has been

described since ancient times. But even more common, though less widely known, is the practice of ant slavery. Apparently what I had been witnessing was a slave raid, not by the black ants, but by the reds.

Both species involved were most likely members of the Formicidae family, the most highly developed of the more than 8,000 recognized ant species. In New England it is common for these red and black ants to build nests adjacent to one another. The black ants are relatively docile insects and normally tolerate the presence of the more aggressive reds in their territory. From time to time, it seems, the red ants make rather well coordinated invasions of the blacks' nests for the purpose of stealing the young larvae. Strangely enough, the blacks offer little if any resistance during these invasions. Most of them remain crouched in the lower levels of their colony (which explains the relative scarcity of blacks visible on their own territory), and the reds generally pay no attention to the black adults, except for the few who try to defend the mounds. These are set upon, as I had observed, until the blacks cease to resist. Unlike out-and-out ant wars, these slave raids result in few deaths on either side.

The black-ant larvae are carried back to the red ants' nest, where a number of them are eaten by the colony. But those that hatch into adults seem to be color-blind to their heredity. Like the legendary white-child captives of raiding Indians, the abducted blacks live out their lives as accepted members of the red colony (though in a somewhat subordinate position), spending most of their time helping to feed and to harvest food for their captors.

Incredible? But then, ants *are* incredible. The eminent French myrmecologist Rémy Chauvin describes their world as "a science-fiction universe." More accurately, perhaps, it is a universe for which science has created fictional handles in order to grasp its mysteries. Ant "warfare," ant "slavery," ant "gardening" and "dairying," ant "armies," even ant "drunkenness" and "drug addiction" have all been described in admirable and precise detail. But these terms seem more revealing of human analogies than of the realities of insect societies, whose superficial similarities to our own only tease us into a recognition of much more profound differences.

Take the "slave raid" I had just witnessed. After some hasty research, I had managed to exchange "warfare" for "slavery," but where was I? A little closer to accurate metaphor, perhaps, but really no closer to the nature of the experience. How passive, for instance, the victims seemed to be, how almost *unaware* of the invaders stealing their young. Was there some hidden benefit the blacks received in return from this practice that made them offer so little resistance? Did the invaders feel masterful, or the invaded downtrodden? Did the captive black larvae feel at all alien in the red society? Do ants *feel* at all, in any remote human sense of the word? Could one imagine an ant abolitionist?

No, these insects were still puzzles, red-and-black hieroglyphs of a summer saga, written in an ancient tongue I had neither the wit nor the perception to read.

4

By late summer a young quail family or two usually makes a brief reappearance in front of the doors. They dash anxiously across the lawn, perhaps feeding on the ants: a pair of large plump adult ideas followed by a string of eight or nine fluffy little afterthoughts. Occasionally, late August brings a brief cool spell, a foretaste of autumn weather. With it the birds seem to revive, and a secondary wave of song is heard on a cool, clear morning, as though everyone suddenly woke up and remembered spring.

Shortly after Labor Day the first of the fall migrants arrive, a few handsome whitethroats, some early juncos, scattered groups of "fall warblers" (drab and anonymous now in their postbreeding plumage), a hermit thrush or winter wren—all appearing suddenly, as though out of nowhere, peeking through the leaves and landing on the lawn through the green curtain, like the next act that has been waiting all summer in the wings.

Then one day, usually in early or mid-September, the grackles arrive, hundreds of dark, iridescent, yellow-eyed blackbirds, their ranks varied with a few redwings, cowbirds, and starling camp followers. For the next few weeks they *occupy* the grounds around my house like black storm troopers, feeding on the abundant supply of acorns in the oaks. My house appears to be on some local flyway for these birds. Every autumn since we have moved in they have bivouacked here, thrashing through the branches and tearing off the nuts from the oak twigs with their long, sharp beaks. All day the roof of the house sounds as though it were being shelled with popgun artillery, and sometimes I have to hold a book or an umbrella over my head to walk to the car.

I see them through the glass doors, threading their dark bodies through the dark leaves like black nets, weaving a violence through the green wall of summer that seems to presage its coming destruction.

From May through September the yard has been a curved proscenium backed by a wide green scrim, with entrance and exit folds everywhere. Here the birds and other summer stock made brief cameo appearances, dressed in the changing costumes of late spring, summer, and early fall, arriving singly, in small groups, or even, like the grackles, in noisy hordes— but always in a defined open space that seemed detached from the deeper world of the woods beyond it, so that they seemed to be displaying themselves for my observation and pleasure alone.

With October, however, the wall of foliage begins to crumble, and the gray maze, like the skeleton behind a mask of green flesh, reasserts itself. There is a rough pattern or sequence to the going of the leaves that, after years of watching, I have learned to recognize but not to count on. In most years the relatively few red maples in the woods go first; I see them blazing here and there on the slopes like scattered red-and-yellow wildfires. Next the pignut hickories, which stood anonymous among the oaks all summer long, turn honey hued and flow clear and distinctive, proclaiming their rich identity. The beeches follow the hickories, as each leaf turns at the outside edges first, then gradually yellows in toward the center, and finally deepens to a uniform butterscotch tan. Each individual beech tree repeats this process, turning color and losing its foliage from the outside in, finally harboring a cluster of coppery leaves close to its trunk all through the winter, like a mound of coals kept covered on the hearth through the night.

The oak leaves are generally the last to turn, and hold on longer when they do. If there are no autumn gales, the first oak leaf may not fall until November. The white oaks in particular will hold on to bunches of crabbed brown leaves all through the stiffest winter winds, refusing to let them go until they are pushed off by next May's buds.

In some years, however, this general sequence gets hopelessly scrambled. One fall the oaks went first, while Virginia creeper was still burning in the red cedars. The maples and hickories were in full color, while on Brewster's main street the locusts and the horse chestnuts—normally the first of all the trees to turn and go—remained leaved and green. For some reason, there were almost no acorns that year, and on December 15 my neighbor's forsythia bloomed. What do we know about seasons anyway?

However it goes, fast or slow, early or late, in small flocks of falling leaves or in mass migrations earthward, the wall of summer eventually dismantles itself, the green tides recede, and, like a developing Polaroid of winter, the far, dipped rim of the kettle hole gradually comes into focus through the maze, revealing a sudden depth and hardness of contour. And as the leaves fall, the windows and doors on the south walls begin to let in not only late-autumn sunshine and a greater sense of exposure but a totally new dimension, even a sense of unreality, to what happens inside.

5

One afternoon in late October, as an easterly blow was building up outside, I was paid a visit by a local town official, a good-hearted soul but a "socializer" who can take an hour to transact five minutes of business. He arrived just before the storm let loose in earnest, placing himself center stage at the table directly in front of the glass doors, where he began to hold forth in that measured, meandering, not unengaging, and even superficially interesting manner that professional talkers seem to have perfected.

I sat opposite him, a captive audience in my own home, half listening, half thinking to myself what a satisfying contrast he formed to the tempest behind him: a crashing bore holding forth as the season and its leaves came crashing down behind him. Every now and then my guest paused momentarily and cast a glance over his shoulder, as though sensing that something was competing with him. But as he looked only for a human face, he saw nothing, and resumed his unending flow of talk with renewed vigor. I sat, nodding, sipping a mug of tea, and thinking to myself how more than one dull play has been saved by a brilliant setting.

After the leaves go completely, the effect can be even more powerful, illuminating our own mortality or that of others. One bright early-winter day, with the sun now very low in the southern sky, my father stopped to visit. He sat in the same place that the inexhaustible talker had occupied, his back also to the glass doors. As we talked quietly over coffee, my eyes, like a light meter, adjusted to the brilliant daylight behind him, so that his figure seemed to darken, lose detail, and become a shrunken silhouette, a mere cutout against the consuming glare of the sky and the cryptic pattern of the shimmering tree branches behind him. My attention must have wandered visibly, for he grew silent and seemed to hunch over slightly, setting down his cooling cup, as though he, too, felt the weight and the power of the light behind him. I had a sudden, overwhelming sense that he was disappearing before my eyes, and felt a painful urge to reach out and draw him back. Instead, I consciously averted my eyes and offered him more coffee.

Dusk is the most powerful time of all at this season. At dinner, with the whole family at the table, I sit at one end, facing the large picture window to the southwest. The sun has just set clear, and the myriad interlaced branches of the oaks grow first dark, then black against the dying light. Then perspective itself goes: the thin limbs cut and weave across one another in a flat plane like a thousand shears, snipping apart the plaited continuities of the day. It is a stark sunset ballet, at once full of terror and peace, as though seen down the long, destroying corridors of the centuries.

If it is not too cold outside, the shades are left up throughout the evening. As night comes on, the black open glass panels finally begin to give us back ourselves, showing us our reflected figures sitting around the lamp at the table, as in so many dark mirrors. Our shapes are somewhat blurred because of the double panes, and this effect plus the darkness give the reflections a kind of distance, as though we saw ourselves on a stage, as people whom we know quite well, whose futures we care about, yet whom we are somehow unable ever to tell what we know about their destinies.

At such times I think we come as close as we ever do to imagining ourselves as we really are, reflected darkly out of the enclosing night. Almost all conversations and meetings in our lives take place out of individual sets of eyes; *we* are never there.

But at such moments we are all there for us to see, fathomless against the dark glass. It is for this sense of ourselves that it gives back to us that I love the night. It confutes our sense of a man-dominated world and throws us back into huddled pin-points of lights and vague ominous glows on the horizon. It gives a return of perspective, dissolving the bounded blue sky of day into a universe of lights rushing away from one another into endless folds of space.

CHAPTER 3

God's Acre

God's Acres once were plenty, the harvest good:
five churchyards, six, in this sparse neighborhood.

—CONRAD AIKEN, "Mayflower"

1
————

Through some quirk of geographical coincidence, I have
spent most of my life living near graveyards. Large tracts of
urban cemeteries covered nearly one-third of the town where
I was born. Since then I have been neighbor to a string of
public and private "parks," cemeteries, churchyards, and family burying grounds of steadily diminishing size, so that I expect
at last to make the acquaintance of a single grave.

Currently I live next door to a small country cemetery that
contains about 150 graves. Red Top Cemetery—or, as it used
to be known less euphemistically, Red Top Graveyard—sits
on a rounded glacial knoll at the intersection of Stony Brook
and Red Top roads. Its half-acre square of land is enclosed by
a plain whitewashed board fence, which I am told was built
by some of its present occupants years ago. Red Top has always
been an unpretentious, even a homely, graveyard. There are
few formal plantings: a single privet hedge in one corner, a

thick stand of lilacs, a few imported yucca plants, and a heaped tangle of multiflora roses gone wild in its center. But its grassy dome is spiked with the tall, thin, crooked columns of black locusts and the dark, tapered-urn shapes of native red cedars, whose natural spacing and contrasting forms give the cemetery an aspect of informal elegance.

Because I was accustomed to cemeteries so early, I have never experienced the unease that many people still feel at having the dead for neighbors. And, as with living neighbors, I have borrowed many things from them at various stages of my life: sledding runs, inspiration for morbid adolescent poetry, trysting places, and information about local communities (deceased natives generally being much more candid and liberal with personal histories than their living relatives are). In the present case, the relationship has grown even more pragmatic. Red Top Cemetery provides me with, among other things, a shortcut to the mailbox, a place where I hide Easter eggs or where my children and their friends sometimes play hide-and-seek among the tombstones, and an added measure of privacy. Occasionally I have salvaged broken or discarded footstones thrown over the fence onto my property, and used them as drainpipe splashboards. It has even occurred to me that my vegetable garden, which lies below the southern slope of the knoll, may benefit to some small degree from the contributions of some of the cemetery's older inhabitants.

For most of the year the little graveyard is left to itself, but each spring a crew from the town highway department shows up for a few days. The workers brush and rake, trim some of the lower branches from the cedars to reveal overgrown gravestones, reset some of the fallen monuments, cut down the lilacs and roses (which grow back again the following year), lime and reseed the bare spots, and in general "spruce it up" for the modest influx of tourists and gravestone rubbers who visit the cemetery each summer.

At the entrance to the cemetery is a sign designating Red Top as an "Ancient Cemetery," an official term signifying that it has been in continuous use for over a hundred years. But those seeking antiquity here are generally disappointed, for it is considerably younger than most of the other small cemeteries in the vicinity.

Red Top's oldest grave bears the comparatively recent date of 1813. It houses no examples of colonial gravestone art, and most of its headstones are small slabs of soft white limestone whose dates and inscriptions have in many cases been eaten away by a century of weather or covered over by yellow-orange splotches of wall lichen that bloom like flattened, slow-growing marigolds across their faces.

No one of great importance is buried here. There are none of the Revolutionary War figures that lie in the old Congregational Church yard in the town center or any of the imposing monuments to nineteenth-century shipping and railroad fortunes that rise out of the large Brewster Cemetery on Lower Road near Cape Cod Bay. Red Top boasts no local luminaries, not even a minister, though it might well have contained one, since for nearly a half century it contained not only graves but also a church.

Near the summit of the knoll, encircled by the untamed tangle of roses that periodically smothers it, a large slab of rough granite rises from the ground. Set into its side is a brass plaque that reads:

SITE OF REFORMED METHODIST CHURCH
(OLD "RED TOP") 1821–1867

Initially, I had surmised that the graveyard had received its name from redtop (*Agrostis alba*), one of the first hay grasses cultivated by the early settlers and whose dark-red flower clusters still rise above the graves in late summer. I later learned that Red Top was in fact named for the old meetinghouse that once stood at the top of the knoll and whose roof shingles were, in the common practice of the day, painted red. The church itself was moved to East Dennis after the Civil War, but the nickname stuck to the churchyard.

No longer a church burying ground, Red Top underwent a somewhat curious history during the next hundred years. It became, according to some accounts, a kind of potter's field, used for the indigent and for "transients"—those who were just passing through but never quite made it. Bearing this out are a number of single stones with names not indigenous to the area—Peck, Goodeno, MacKenzie. But the graveyard also continued to be used by those local families whose members had belonged to the Methodist congregation, as well as by some who had not. It seems in time to have become something almost unique in this area—not strictly a parish, family, or town cemetery, but a real "neighborhood" burying ground.

The property continued to be listed on the tax rolls as belonging to something called the "Red Top Cemetery Association," though whatever care it received came from nearby residents who scythed the family plots and kept the poison ivy from creeping over the fence. In 1975 the East Dennis congregation formally gave up all claims to Red Top Cemetery and the town of Brewster assumed maintenance of, though not title to, the property. One might say, in the language of the town assessors, that it belongs to "owners unknown."

2
———

Bereft of its church, modest in size and antiquity, devoid of unique folk art, and lacking in historical importance, this small cemetery is usually passed over by hsitory buffs and curiosity seekers. Yet its rows of unpretentious markers, all facing the setting sun, possess a shared, if commonplace, humanity. Read in their entirety, they give some sense of the general makeup of this community in the past. Legends and dates suggest something of the tenor of the times, while individual stones or groups of monuments often provide fragments of personal or family histories.

One summer I thought it might be interesting to take an informal census of these mute neighbors of mine. Over the course of the season I found 140 stones that still possessed legible names and dates. The great majority are dominated by a handful of local families. Searses lead all others with 38, followed by 14 Ellises, a dozen Blacks, and a sprinkling of Howlands, Howes, Crowells, and Clarks—good West Brewster names all.

Demographically, the dates on the headstones are typical of their age and place. The average age of those buried in Red Top Cemetery works out to 43.6 years, roughly the national life expectancy during the late nineteenth century. Comparatively few, however, actually died in middle age. A relatively high infant mortality (8 percent) is balanced at the other end by a surprising longevity. Of those who survived infancy and early childhood diseases, nearly half lived to be over sixty, over a third reached seventy, and eighteen became octogenarians and nonagenarians, led by the venerable Dorcas Howland, who died in 1939, at the age of ninety-nine. The tough endured.

Of those who died in their twenties and thirties, most were wives in their childbearing years. Fifteen died in adolescence, most likely from smallpox, typhus, or tuberculosis. Of this last group, one stone in particular drew my attention. It belonged to Mahala Tobey, who died in 1827, at the age of thirteen. Not only did she die at the very brink of adolescence, but she seems to have been laid to rest among strangers. No other members of her family are buried with her.

Out of the blurred legends and truncated stones, many of them skewed like crooked teeth by over a century of frost, one hears or half hears certain attitudes or emotions shared by those who lie here, as well as hints of personal tragedy. The remarkably uniform and modest size of all the headstones bespeaks either a Methodist aversion to ostentation or, more likely, a certain economic democracy in the community. Where the family could afford a carving, it is usually the standard willow-and-urn of the Victorian era, but even these decorations are few. Inscriptions are more numerous. There are a few of the earlier *memento mori* ("As I was once, so you must be") variety. More common are sentimental references to "this vale of tears" or "this world of woe," to children as "faded blossoms," and to "meeting again" in the afterlife.

Most of the epitaphs, with their conventional expressions of grief, exhortations to virtue, and professions of faith, are such as can be found in almost any cemetery of its vintage. Yet some of the headstones bear the distinct mark of the Cape and its ocean-going heritage. There are at least half a dozen graves of young men "drown'd" or "lost at sea," including one boy of eight. On these, one occasionally catches a glimpse of a more candid emotion, as on the stone of Leonard, son of Moody and Jane Sears, who was lost off Provincetown at the age of eighteen in the schooner *Bride* during the legendary and fatal gale of October 3, 1841:

> Tho' I was drown'd in yonder waves,
> Beneath this stone I sleep;
> While some of my companions dear
> Now lie beneath the deep.

Though they are written in the first person, the lines convey the bleak comfort taken by the victim's family in having been spared the more common lot of those whose sons were lost at sea—the empty grave.

The most common epitaphs of all are such laconic comments as "Baby Has Gone," "At Rest," "No More Sorrow," "Blessed Are the Dead," and "All Is Well." Whatever these words lack in eloquence or originality is more than made up for in the simple power of authenticity of the accompanying names and dates. Here is a representative sample:

In memory of Daniel S. Crowell
son of Capt. Danel & Ruth Crowell,
who died Aug. 13, 1837, aged 2 years.

In memory of William P. Crowell,
son of Capt. Daniel & Ruth Crowell,
who died Aug. 28, 1838, aged 7 years.

In memory of Ruth Crowell,
wife of Capt. Daniel Crowell,
who died Sept. 29, 1838, aged 30 years.

In general the risks and strains of the open deck and the field seem to have been less fatal than those of the birthing room and the kitchen. Husbands, especially ship captains, tended to outlive their wives, and many a man went through more than one spouse in his lifetime. Isaac Crowell, for instance, had two wives, who gave him three children, all of whom died before he did. Thatcher Clark outlasted three spouses and finally had himself buried next to his first wife, setting the latter two a discreet distance away.

Then there is Capt. Freeman Sears, who, it seems, could not live unmarried. He went through four wives in his eighty years, beginning with Hitty, three years his senior, followed by Mary, four years his junior, Patty, twelve years his senior, and finally Sally, eighteen years his junior. Having sampled all this chronological variation, he eventually died in 1879, surrounding himself with his last three wives and leaving poor Hitty, for some reason, alone on the other side of the hill.

After so many examples of linear polygamy and patriarchal control of final domestic arrangements, it was somehow gratifying to come upon the stone of Deziah Hutchins, wife of John Hutchins (1844–1913). When John died, Deziah, in the practice of the day, added her own name and incomplete dates below those of her husband,

DEZIAH C. HUTCHINS
1841–19

presumably in anticipation of following him shortly. That is how the stone still reads today. It would appear that Deziah, at least, managed to escape.

3
———

What sets Red Top off from most of its "ancient" counterparts is that it is no mere historical artifact but a living cemetery, a continuing part of this community that is still occasionally used for its original purpose. Every year or two a new burial takes place, though the number of available spaces is growing quite small. I have a friend whose small daughter is buried here, and another whose parents were interred next to my property line a few years ago. It has occurred to me that I might someday set off a plot of my own land that abuts the cemetery for future use, but I am not ready yet for such final commitments.

One winter afternoon, shortly after Christmas, I took a shortcut through the cemetery on my way back from the mailbox. Warm, blinding sun poured down on the soft untouched snow, the dark green cedars shone in winter splendor like large, fat candles in front of the stark, furrowed, twisted locusts. The stones sat in little wind-carved hollows, their gray-blue shadows curving away over the snow like shark fins. Some of the smaller white tombstones leaned against the shaggy cedar trunks, as though snuggling up to them for shelter and comfort.

At this time of the year, the little cemetery is brightened by a scattering of wreaths, bows, and other holiday decorations, several of them intricately fashioned from native greenery and cones by friends and relatives still living in the area. Most of these were placed on the newer graves over in the northwest corner, but on the south side, near the white wooden fence, an elderly white-haired woman in a bright red coat was arranging a wreath on an old grave with her foot. I went over to say hello and to see whether I might help. She smiled and told me that this was the grave of her first husband, Augustus, who died in 1935. He lies buried with his first wife, who died twenty years before him. Though long since remarried, she has lived her entire life in the village of East Dennis, about a mile to the west. The wreath had been formed from a simple spray of cedar sprigs, bright with clusters of electric-blue berries and fastened together with a plastic red bow.

What struck me, talking with her, was not just that after nearly half a century she still came to lay a wreath on her first husband's grave but also that she still *could* do it, that through a sustained proximity rare in our day, she was still able to pay remembrance to an old affection after so many years. In an age of human scatterings, this seemed a continuity in league with life, not death.

After she left, I stayed awhile, walking around to look at the other decorations, almost all of which were on the newer graves. The woman's husband was the only person I found who had died before 1950 who was still remembered by the living. All the others lay alone and unvisited.

To comfort someone, probably myself, I borrowed a sprig of winterberry from one of the newer wreaths, broke off a small sprig of cedar from a living tree, and, with a bit of dried grass picked up from the snowless circle beneath it, fashioned a crude decoration of my own. I walked over and placed it on the snow-covered grave of Mahala Tobey, Aet. 13.

4
————

Late last summer there was a burial in Red Top that occasioned a more general notice in the town than this little cemetery has been accustomed to. Brewster's first police chief,

Earl Folger, had died at the age of seventy-eight and was to be laid to rest with full municipal honors.

The ex-chief had been hospitalized and "in a bad way" for most of the summer. About a week before he died, I saw his wife walking with the town archivist in Red Top. He was helping her pick out a grave site. As usual in these small older cemeteries, they had to be careful of unmarked graves. Before each burial here it used to be a common practice to have one of the older residents come down and look over the prospective plot to make sure the new grave was not going in over an old one. A few years ago, however, an official inventory was made from town records, and presumably all the bodies in the grave-yard are now "mapped." But there is always a possibility of error, and a few days later a man from the local funeral home came out and carefully probed the chosen site with long, thin, screw-tipped steel rods. It was clean.

There is something fascinating and refreshing in this straightforward poking about in the ground for old bodies. It is one of those primitive and direct measures still occasionally required in our relationship with the earth, as when the high-way crew abandons its mowing machines and hand-scythes some of the steeper roadside slopes.

Early on the morning of the interment, several town work-ers arrived to give Red Top a quick and somewhat rough hair-cut, replace some of the rotted posts, prop up one of the old headstones that regularly falls over, and remove one entire sec-tion of fence along Stony Brook Road at the "new corner."

When I went out to post some letters at about nine o'clock, the town crew had finished its work, and two young men from the funeral home had arrived in a pickup truck full of tools. They were carefully removing squares of sod above the grave site with spades and placing them in neat stacks on a piece of canvas laid out beside it. When they were finished, a backhoe arrived on a flatbed truck, entered through the gap in the fence, and began digging the hole.

The job took about an hour. After the machine had dug the rough hole, the gravediggers climbed down into it and squared off the sides and the bottom. When completed, the grave was eight feet long, four feet wide, and the traditional six feet deep at the upper end, though only about five feet deep at the lower end because of the slope of the knoll. The excavated material, all of it light, coarse sand, had been laid on the canvas next to the sod squares, and both sand and sod were now covered neatly with a tarpaulin of bright green Astroturf. Rough planks had been set around the perimeter of the grave in order to support the metal bier that lay a little way up the hill. The bier was a rather ingenious device, designed like a litter. Its frame was made of thick chromed-steel rods with nylon webbing woven across them. The side rods were constructed to rotate by means of a crank inserted into one of the metal balls in the corners, thus allowing the casket to be smoothly lowered on the nylon straps.

The workers had now gone off to lunch, and I stood by the graveside, looking at the fringe of grass around the opening, the thin layer of topsoil below the rim, the thicker layer of subsoil beneath, darkly stained with leached minerals, and the long, straight walls of soft, yellow sand pocked here and there with small, protruding rocks. The flat dirt bottom was tracked with the fresh footprints of the diggers. It seemed totally devoid of morbidity, a place, if not exactly inviting, at least clean, comfortable, and unthreatening—more like something children might dig on a beach than a solemn grave. The Cape below, it appeared, was not so different from the Cape above, and the move seemed hardly a radical one.

Earlier, one of the workers had expressed some concern about whether the ceremony, which was set for three o'clock, would come off on schedule. They were still awaiting the arrival of the metal vault, which was being shipped down from Boston. One of the fuel tanks at the Cape Cod Canal generating plant had exploded that morning, closing the bridges to all traffic for several hours, and the truck was apparently still held up.

By one o'clock, however, when I went out to get the mail, the vault had arrived. It looked like a huge sarcophagus, nearly eight feet long and made of thick, decorated, copper-plated steel. For a while it lay open and unattended by the side of Stony Brook Road, its lid off to one side, as though some minor resurrection had taken place. I wondered about the purpose of such a massive container. As far as I could see, its primary function would be to keep the coffin from rotting and the grave above it from sinking in, a contingency for which one used to provide by mounding the dirt up slightly above a new grave. State sanitary codes assert that raw sewage is purified enough to drink by leaching through only four feet of soil; surely a human body cannot be that much more corrupt! At any rate, I felt I would not want to be so utterly sealed off from both life *and* death.

Soon the men from the funeral home returned, this time with a front-end loader. The vault, which must have weighed nearly a ton, was hoisted by the bucket on a thick chain, wheeled into the cemetery, and carefully maneuvered down into the hole. The planks around the edge were then covered with more strips of Astroturf, the bier was set in place over the opening, and all was finally ready.

A little before three, having changed into a clean shirt, I walked out by way of my neighbor's driveway, which runs along the back of the cemetery by a stone wall. At this point I was growing a little uneasy about my position as disinterested observer, but I had followed things this far and didn't want to miss the central event. I decided I would remain outside the wall, in the drive, during the ceremony.

It was a still, hot August afternoon. Cicadas droned metallically in the overarching locust trees, and in the shade beneath them two women sat fanning themselves on the stone wall. One was a neighbor from down the road, who said that it had been just too hot to go into Orleans for the funeral. She introduced her friend, who had been a police matron under the late chief and had come down all the way from New Hampshire for the service. The raised bier, now in place above the grave, was surrounded by mounds of flowers.

Presently the funeral entourage began to arrive. The hearse came first, followed by family cars and a police escort of six vehicles—Brewster's entire fleet. Stony Brook Road was blocked off to traffic, and only a single patrolman remained on duty, sitting in one of the cruisers to stay in touch with the station by radio. Four officers carried the magnificent polished maple coffin into the cemetery while the rest formed an honor guard for family, friends, and town officials to pass through. There were about thirty mourners altogether, a gathering of unusual size and formal dignity for this small old churchyard.

Yet the graveside service itself was simple and traditional, no doubt much like those that had been repeated here many times over the last two centuries. It seemed to reaffirm Red Top's role as a living part of this community, and for that alone it was affecting. I found myself wishing I had known the deceased better, or at least had held some minor town position during his tenure as chief that might have let me come out from behind the screen of trees and take a rightful place among the mourners. But I was merely the next-door neighbor, watching the new family move in. I would make my acquaintances later.

When the service was over and the American flag draping the coffin had been folded and presented to the widow by the current police chief, the minister announced that everyone was invited to the family home for refreshments. I stayed, after the last vehicle had departed, to watch the coffin being lowered into the grave. I have often wondered why this is no longer done during the service. It would seem to be an appropriate part of it, especially during the "ashes to ashes, dust to dust" portion. Instead, when these lines were read the undertaker stepped discreetly up to the coffin and poured a vial of what looked like chalk powder over its top.

It struck me as incomplete and a little evasive to have everyone leave when the coffin and its contents were still above ground, but I soon discovered there is a practical reason for this. Lowering a modern casket down into its vault is a tricky process requiring a good deal of vocal as well as physical maneuvering that would have been out of place during the burial service. A few minutes after the last vehicle had left, the two gravediggers reappeared with their pickup, and the two undertakers who had remained removed their dark suitcoats to join them in the work of finishing up. Besides lowering the coffin, this involved setting the vault lid in place (it took all four of them to wrestle the lid over to the graveside, where it was attached to a chain pulley on a tripod and lowered), filling the grave in by hand, replacing the sod, and loading planks, bier, Astroturf, and other equipment back onto their truck.

They seemed quite at ease in their labor. Even the undertakers quickly lapsed from professional gravity into traditional gravedigger jocularity with remarks such as what a great afternoon it would have been to commit a robbery in Brewster. When they began shoveling in the dirt, I left. From the house, I could still hear them going at it at five o'clock. Putting a person in the ground, it seems, is a full day's work.

Shortly before sunset I walked once more over to the new grave. The truck was gone and everything had been cleaned up. The ground was again smooth and flat, the excess dirt had been carted away, and the squares of sod had been so carefully replaced that it was nearly impossible to tell where the grass had been disturbed. Only the flowers now mounded over the grave and the small temporary funeral-home marker staked at one end gave any indication of what had taken place here or who the new occupant was. Earl Folger had passed seamlessly and in good order into the earth.

5
———

Summer is gone. No more tourists come to rub the plain slate and limestone tablets or to look in vain among their rows for some odd antiquity. Now, in the first glorious, clean wave of autumn weather, the seasonal emptiness is transparent, restoring a certain old honesty of countenance to this country graveyard. The grass, no longer mowed, grows long like Whitman's "uncut hair of graves" and sends up red-topped seedstalks that bend in concert in the soft, southeast breeze. Small locust leaves lie scattered, curled and brown, over the crest of the knoll, and the yuccas thrust their dry, rattling seedpods high above drooping clusters of leaf spears.

I am here finishing up my survey of Red Top's inhabitants, accompanied today by my four-year-old daughter. Still tan and blond from the summer, she runs barefoot among the headstones while I collect carved names and dates. At one point, as I kneel in front of one of the stones, trying to decipher its eroded epitaph, she prances over and asks, "What are the plastic flowers for?"

"Well, people put them there to honor—to remember friends and relatives they knew who have died."

She jumps up on one of the low footstones and balances there: "Like my gerbil?"

"Yes—sort of." I wonder whether an Important Talk is coming up.

"And—if they love them and—[she struggles here with a new word] and *miss* them?"

"Yes, that's right—that's very good."

"You know, sometimes when people die you get to have their

things," she says, jumping down and running off again before I have a chance to temper this bit of candor.

She chases after a song sparrow that is in one of the flame-shaped cedars. Round and round the tree she runs, while the bird hops about on the needleless inner branches, as though inside a cage it knows she can't get into.

Strange impulses surface on such a day, in such a place. The heart is prompted to a kind of joyful melancholy. When we were walking over here from the house, I held her hand and noticed for the first time that I could stand straight up without feeling any pull from her on my arm. How many children, I wonder, have I pulled up by the hand in my lifetime? Two? Twenty? After the first, the rest are legion.

Should I introduce her to Mahala Tobey? Or take her over to the grave of my neighbor's daughter? *Here*, I might say, *is a little girl who died when she was your age. Here are people, or what they come to. Here are*—ah, but then she comes back and takes my hand, leading me out of this settling, self-indulgent intro-spection, away from the past, toward some new discovery she has made. I rise up and follow her to the other side of the hill, where she points toward the ground. There, between the stalks of grass and plantain leaves, is a tiny cedar seedling, barely two inches tall, a fist-sized cluster of sharp, spiky needles—like some bristly moss or dwarf cactus—that has survived repeated mowings.

"Look at the baby Christmas tree," she says.

CHAPTER *4*

Entering the Garden

1

April again. Under a mixed sky of brilliant sun and low, racing clouds, I have come down to the garden this morning to plant the first peas of the year. The fresh-tilled earth lies clean before me, spread out and waiting for me to begin tattooing this year's design on its unblemished skin.

Late last fall, after the first frost, I finally dug up the rest of the potatoes, composted the tomato vines and the cornstalks, covered the remaining carrots with mulch, and pulled up the last of the onions, leaving them to dry in the sun a few days before bringing them into the house to braid and hang from the ceiling rafters. Then, in February, I purged the garden, burning a huge pile of brush and old tires in its center, scorching the ground to a gray scab and scattering the ashes into the soil.

Now the year has come round again, and the ground lies freshly turned, rank and dark with the compost of the year mixed back into its loam. A large mound of marsh grass, recently gathered off the beach, is piled up next to the fence for later mulching. Nearby, in the workshed, lettuce and tomato seedlings incubate on window shelves in Styrofoam egg cartons. During the past week the soil has dried out so that it no longer compacts into oozy mud in my grasp, but crumbles like chocolate cake. All lies in readiness; and yet, at the gate, I pause.

Most gardens, like most marriages, are begun in innocence: full of high expectations, an intoxicating sense of independence, and a passion for possession. A garden is something we seek to cordon off from nature, to make over in our own image, to give a human shape to, as part of the unfinished earth. At the very least we tend to think of it as a kind of personal statement, and so we take umbrage, and then action, when disease, weeds, and pests mangle, chew, and rot our well-formed and articulated rows. In this sense, gardening is often our first step out of a strictly human enclosure into a wider field. It is in many cases the closest we get to wilderness, for it contains a surprising amount of potential confrontation and unexpected contact, drawing us deeply and often unwillingly into the ritual of the year.

I remember a soft May evening during the first year I had a garden here, only a few weeks after the bulldozer had plucked up the pitch-pine stumps like giant, inverted carrots from the site and dug the larger boulders like huge, petrified potatoes out of the raw ground. I was inside the house when suddenly the gentle piping of the spring peepers was pierced by a loud, prolonged squeal that filled the air and tightened my bones. I froze, for it sounded at first like the scream of a very young child. It came again, a high-pitched *eep! eep! eep!*, more animallike this time and from the direction of the garden.

Rushing out of the house and down to the edge of the dark square of earth, I could make out the gray form of our cat somewhere in the middle. He had something in his paws, which he would release and catch again in his deadly manner of play. It was a baby rabbit, a tiny frightened thing no more than five inches long. When the cat pounced once more with sheathed claws, the rabbit let out again that pitiful, humanlike squeal. An irrational anger welled up in me; picking up a stone, I drove the villain off into the night.

The tiny rabbit, scared to death, flattened itself with its ears back, close to the ground, breathing rapidly and shallowly. It looked steadily at me with large, black BB eyes, but would not move at all until I prodded it with my finger. It had such touching faith in its limited subterfuge, so new and untried, so undamaged by experience. Yet it was so full of terror, so tense with holding it in, that it seemed it might literally die of fright. Nothing so vulnerable, I thought, should have to be so terrified, so desperate to escape. It ought rather to flow willingly, with easy acceptance, toward whatever inevitably stalked it, as I have seen tiny, schooling fish fry wheeling calmly in the currents toward the dark, waiting, gaping maw of an eel.

That night I kept the cat in; but as spring wore on and the lettuce began to come up in our unfenced garden, I found myself letting him out in the evenings with less compunction and more philosophy. After all, many of the rabbit's natural predators had been displaced by my own and my neighbors' presence, and the cat was only in some sense replacing them. Later I would lie in bed thinking such thoughts, as a series of high, small, final screams punctuated the night air, bringing me visions of rabbit skulls being crunched in the bower of cat-brier next to the garden.

2
———

The following year I put up a rabbit fence that, true to its name, kept out rabbits, though little else. Raccoons climbed the fence and dug up the fish I had placed under the corn hills;

chipmunks slipped through it and ate my strawberries; some of the local deer stepped right over it and nibbled the tender corn shoots. And, of course, no one has yet invented a garden fence for insects.

Every man must come to terms with insects in his garden, for they form the most certain and most numerous of his relationships there. If nothing else, he will learn some facts of which he might otherwise have remained contentedly ignorant. I have discovered, for instance, that the glistening, bronzed bodies of Japanese beetles show up not only on other people's roses but on my pole beans as well, that corn-borer eggs are deposited on the young ears at night by undistinguished pale brown moths, and that it is the field crickets which, in late summer, eat my ripe tomatoes. I have also been forced to grant, if not the virtue, at least the undeniable convenience of certain pesticides, and have even managed to learn something about their individual components and relative effectiveness.

My own role in these insect relationships is determined by the abundance of the insect and the nature of the crop affected. If the crop is one not particularly vital to the overall yield of the garden or if it is not noticeably affected by the insect's presence, I usually allow myself the luxury of passive observation and speculation.

Sunflowers are a good example of a spectator crop. I grow them each year primarily for their towering beauty and for their seeds, which provide free bird food. Not being a staple crop, they are often planted late and may not blossom until late August. They show great variation in growth, from thirty-inch midgets to superb giants with hard, hairy green stems over an inch thick and hyperpituitary composite blossoms that nod well over eight feet above the earth.

Both the stalks of these plants and the large elephant-ear leaves that protrude from them are usually covered with hundreds of small leafhoppers, sucking insects less than half an inch long, with humped, raised wings that form a ridge down their backs when closed. Most are reddish brown with white transverse bands, while others are pale lime green—species I have tentatively identified as the three-banded and the potato leafhopper, respectively. They spend the late-summer days sucking the juices from the stalk and both sides of the leaves. At times they are so thick that they appear from a distance like some dark mold on the plants. In some areas of the country they are considered serious garden pests, but they have never done my sunflowers any significant harm.

The interesting thing about these leafhoppers is that, like aphids, they are constantly tended and shepherded about by larger ants, black in color with reddish abdomens, which scurry unceasingly from one flock to another, stroking the leafhoppers and checking up on them. When it rains, they actively herd the sucking insects to the undersides of the leaves, as a farmer might drive his cattle into a barn during a storm, where they remain dry and protected until the sun reappears and they are driven out to graze again. Also as with aphids, the ants reputedly "farm" these insects for their "honeydew"—a sweet, sticky substance exuded from the leafhoppers' abdomens—and may provide their "flocks" some protection from predators.

In describing this example of insect "husbandry," I have blithely employed the same convenient, however suspect, human metaphors used earlier to interpret the ant "war." In such cases I can allow my curiosity to be as casual as I like, for I have no real stake in the outcome. In most situations involving garden insects, however, I am required to play a more active and judgmental role. When borers and earwigs show up in the cornsilk, when hornworms attack the tomatoes and potato bugs proliferate, when a lone caterpillar begins singlemandibularly devouring an entire row of young lettuce, it is time not to watch but to do something.

Of all the creatures in my garden there is none with whom I have formed a more active and intimate relationship than the cabbage-worm butterfly, *Pieris rapae*. From late spring all through the hot dog days of August, these small butterflies dance tirelessly, flitting crookedly on ash-white wings over cabbage, broccoli, and cauliflower, as well as the border nasturtiums.

Introduced in this country over a hundred years ago, they now range from Central America to Alaska. Like most butterflies, they are sexually dimorphic: the female has an extra pair of sooty markings on her wings. As their common name indicates, however, their primary interest for gardeners lies not with the rather undistinguished-looking adult but with the larval form.

For years I had watched the adult butterflies dancing and twirling through the summer months over fields and gardens, observing them with casual, ignorant pleasure, not even knowing their names. When I came to garden myself, however, I learned that this graceful dalliance, left unchecked, soon resulted in dozens of soft, fuzzy, inch-long, pale green caterpillars that quickly consumed all my broccoli leaves, on which their camouflage is perfect.

There are sprays for cabbage worms, of course, and when an infestation has become particularly severe (usually owing to my own negligence), I have on occasion resorted to a bacterial insecticide. Normally, though, not that many worms are on the plants, and instead of spraying them I employ a method I learned from a friend of mine. He educates them.

Educating cabbage worms is a simple, but extremely effective, method of training them to stay off broccoli plants. It consists of placing one's index finger directly above the larva to be instructed and one's thumb under the leaf directly beneath it, and then pinching firmly. As my friend assured me, "It always works. They never come back."

Not only does it work, but educating the cabbage worms has also made me a part of the butterflies' dance. Early in the morning, before the sun comes up over the trees, I go out into the garden and train a dozen or so larvae off the broccoli leaves.

Their bright mint-jelly guts squirt out one end, leaving their flattened skins to shrivel and blacken on the leaves, where they attract flies.

When I have finished instructing them, I retire to the porch and watch the winged adults hopping and pirouetting over the partially chewed plants. Frequently they fly in pairs, twirling and shifting about some common, invisible axis, like some airborne strand of DNA. At first I thought this might be some kind of primitive lepidopteran mating flight, or pair-bonding ritual, similar to the courtship flights of terns and other shorebirds. But one day, venturing out into the garden at high noon, I watched a pair of butterflies separate and land on different plants. Each had the extra pair of sooty wing spots that marks the female, and each gripped the edge of the leaf with her front pair of legs, curving her abdomen down and under to deposit her eggs on the bottom side of the broccoli leaf. The eggs were pale yellow ovoids, barely a millimeter long. Only two or three were deposited in one spot, but each female seemed capable of laying several dozen at a stretch. I noticed that, when laid on a young broccoli head, the eggs were virtually invisible on the yellow nubs of the developing buds.

Sometimes I will try to quicken the tempo of our dance by scraping the new eggs off the leaves as soon as they are laid. But this is a tedious and lengthy task, and the heat of midday soon drives me back to the porch, where I sit, drinking lemonade in the shade, as once more the cabbage butterflies go dancing and twirling out over the garden, depositing more tiny eggs. Then, late in the afternoon, I go out once again to administer another lesson to some of the more tardy or thick-skinned worms.

So we move contrapuntally through the summer days—the butterflies, the worms, and I—locked in the ritualized steps of some formal dance: pinch, twirl, dip, scrape; pinch, twirl, scrape.

3
___

Despite such encounters, however, the new gardener generally escapes many ills, and is subject to a false sense of exception. His first summer is usually weedless, and most insect pests do not show up until the second or third year. During my first few growing seasons, I received only such minor and indirect jolts to my crops and my environmental philosophy as I have already described, but I suppose I knew all along that it was only a matter of time before the woodchucks found me out.

There is a good population of woodchucks in most areas of Cape Cod, and my neighborhood is no exception. Often I have found their burrows on my walks and, when driving, have seen their squat, brown, furry forms loping off into the brush beside the roads.

Several of my neighbors had been plagued with them at one time or another. Only the summer before last one poor fellow, possessing one of the best gardens around, had been the victim of a particularly persistent beast. Fences four feet high and buried a foot in the earth had failed to deter it, and his entire bean crop had been taken twice. He asked me whether I knew anything about woodchucks. Not having been bothered myself that year by anything worse than cabbage worms and weeds, I cheerfully passed on what little I knew about them and their prowess in overcoming human obstacles—experiencing, I'm afraid, a measure of that perverse pleasure that always seems to accompany our sympathy toward those misfortunes of others that we, in a similar situation, have managed to escape.

Despite the devastation to his garden, however, he was as yet reluctant to employ more "permanent" solutions to his woodchuck problem, though I could see that his humane impulses were under increasing stress. I promised I would find out what I could for him and report back. Fired with a sense of altruistic mission, I hunted down the beast in several reference books on mammals and found that the woodchuck is a member of the squirrel and marmot family, order Rodentia, a solitary animal eighteen to twenty-five inches long and weighing about ten pounds. It digs winding, chambered burrows that can be up to forty feet in length and are usually built into hillsides, slanted upward to keep them dry. "Here its blind young are born," said one source, "up to 9 in number; a few weeks later they play by the mound of fresh earth at the burrow entrance, where the adults also like to take an occasional sunbath."

A few days later I visited my gardener friend again. To the top of his already-high fence, he was adding another strip of chicken wire, this one leaning outward from the garden on wooden supports to form a continuous lip around its perimeter, which he hoped the chuck would not be able to climb. I reported my findings and told him that the only mention of woodchuck prevention I had come across was a somewhat complacent statement to the effect that their destructive reputation was greatly exaggerated and that "in fact, woodchucks do relatively little damage to truck gardens." From the look he gave me, I knew he found my report less than satisfactory. I sympathized, but felt I had done my neighborly duty. And so, leaving him hammering away in the hot sun, I went home and enjoyed a chuckless summer.

The following spring, last year, I spent a good deal of time and effort preparing the garden soil, digging out by hand all of the stones and boulders over which the Rototiller had happily bounced the year before, working in the compost and peat moss, hauling in carloads of salt hay for mulch and constructing a tight, new gate for our modest barrier of rabbit fencing.

April was surprisingly sunny, May generous with rain, and by the second week in June I made a first, tentative harvest of a few handfuls of leaf lettuce. The peas had reached a lush, two-foot-high tangle, the tomatoes were beginning to put out blossoms, the iceberg-lettuce plants continued to head up in the cool June weather, and at the back of the garden the first spiraling pole-bean tendrils had just begun their long, twisting ascent up the large wooden frame I had built for them that year. I left, feeling pleased with the pact I had made with the earth here.

Late that afternoon I went out to the garden again to see whether it needed watering and found that devastation had arrived—by way of a small, freshly dug hole beneath a side section of fencing. The broccoli was completely gone, along with much of the lettuce. Half of the wax-bean row had been eaten to the ground, as though a mower had gone over it and stopped short. The peas, like a green wave spilled, had been dragged to the ground and nibbled extensively. The bush beans had also been heavily grazed, and against the wooden frame the stems of the pioneer pole-bean plants were now bare, leaf-less wires curled forlornly around their support strings.

I stood there taking in the scene and feeling anger involuntarily well up inside me. Yet beneath my anger I could imagine the wonder that the beast must have felt upon first entering and surveying the variegated feast it had stumbled on. I could see it, beginning methodically and thoroughly at first, devouring the broccoli, then the peas, then moving on to the wax beans, where, halfway through, it had apparently given in to the intoxication of plenty and rambled about, like a child left alone in a candy store, sampling everything as fast as it could.

What bothered me most, somehow, was that it had gone about its destruction so unsurreptitiously, so brazenly, in broad daylight, with me awake inside the house not a hundred feet away, as though it had a perfect right to its plunder, to the fruits of *my* labor, and could not imagine any enmity directed against itself.

Well, there it was, another blow to my illusion of a charmed life. Now what? Books, as I had already discovered, had little to offer in the way of advice. Asking around, I soon discovered that any neighborhood containing both gardens and wood-chucks possesses an enormous fund of local woodchuck lore, of which the newly afflicted soon becomes the beneficiary. Everyone willingly (almost *eagerly*, it seemed) offered his or her own woodchuck story and recommendation.

The gun was most frequently recommended as the surest solution, but I neither owned nor knew how to use one. One friend offered to come over and shoot the beast for me, though I must not tell anyone, he said, since he had his reputation as a conservationist to protect. Some of the old-timers, I was told, used to stuff kerosene-soaked rags down the animal's burrow and light them, while others suggested the more contemporary store-bought "woodchuck bombs," which turn the burrow into a lethal gas chamber.

Others offered less extreme solutions. Hav-A-Hart traps were recommended, though woodchuck-size traps are expensive and I had some doubts about their effectiveness. As with many other territorial creatures, there is usually a floating population of nonbreeding individuals in the vicinity ready to move into one chuck's territory if it is removed. Besides, would I want someone trapping *his* woodchucks and releasing them in *my* part of town?

Moreover, I did not wish to confront or remove the animal if I did not have to, merely keep it out. A dog kept on the premises discourages chucks, I was told. I didn't want a dog. Someone suggested moving the garden closer to the house. I gave him a look. Well, then, there were always electric fences.

One neighbor mentioned that he had had success burying two feet of chicken wire a few inches below the ground outside the fence, the idea being that the woodchuck, trying to burrow beneath the fence, hits the wire, isn't smart enough to begin digging further back, and eventually gets discouraged. And so, despite the woodchuck's reputed climbing ability, I went to the hardware store, bought eighteen dollars' worth of chicken wire, and spent two hot, muggy afternoons clearing the brier-choked perimeter of our garden, pick-and-shoveling out dozens more stones, laying the wire, attaching it to the bottom of the fence, and covering it over with soil again. Then I propped the peas back up on their brush, replanted the wax beans, and hoped that the lettuce might recover on its own if left unmolested. It had been a lot of work, but it was done. And none too soon, either, as I had seen signs of tentative digging around the fence while I was working.

For several days after I buried the chicken wire, no new devastation appeared in the garden. The woodchuck had apparently been foiled by this tactic, and I congratulated myself that peaceful coexistence had been restored by such a simple (if somewhat costly) measure.

Soon, however, self-congratulation began to turn to suspicion. The pole beans simply sat there and refused to climb up their frame. The peas did not blossom. The lettuce did not appear to have been eaten further, but neither had it made a comeback. Was it just the dry weather, or was the woodchuck still around, taking only enough each day that I did not notice it? Yet I could find no new burrows inside the garden or even any signs of attempted burrowing outside it.

During the next few days, suspicion grew into paranoia. I began to inspect the plants minutely: Had that pea plant been nibbled before? Was that broccoli chewed down like that earlier? And yet, the untouched half-row of wax beans remained untouched—I thought. Still . . .

After another week had passed, I could fool myself no longer. The chuck was undoubtedly making daily appearances, apparently climbing over the fence and keeping most of the greens in the garden trimmed back at a pace that kept up with their growth. It was, in fact, harvesting my crops in accordance with good conservation principles, taking what is called the "maximum sustainable yield."

Once again I was the beneficiary of local woodchuck lore, eagerly offered by friends and neighbors. Ah yes, chucks were expert climbers. One neighbor had seen them clamber with ease over six-foot fences. Another had actually watched one climbing up her bean poles and nibbling the beans off the top. Truly extraordinary.

I began to look for the den. I was not exactly sure what I would do if I located it, but the area around the garden was thickly wooded and I had no success. Right next to the garden was a large brush pile I had heaped up earlier that spring, and one afternoon I noticed a strong animal odor coming from it. Someone had told me that when a woodchuck finds a good eating spot it is likely to take up residence close by. The idea that the creature was not only harvesting my crops in broad daylight but also living right next to them in a ready-made home of my own creation was infuriating. I spent several hours moving the entire brush pile by hand but got nothing for my labors except scratched hands and pitch-covered clothes.

What further "preventive" measures could I take? Higher fences? Barbed wire? Electrified fencing? Armed guards? Radar? How much was a garden worth? Was the woodchuck trying to tell me something? Coexistence came harder than I had thought.

In addition to the woodchuck lore I had gathered, I was surprised by the number of stories of human savagery that these animals provoked: of the young boy who rushed into his father's garden and kicked one to death; of the man who set his German shepherd on one and stood watching it tear the beast to pieces; of the woman who, while working one day in her garden, saw a chuck climb over the fence and begin placidly chewing on her lettuce a few yards away. Such audacity was too much. She banged it over the head with a shovel and hung its body by its tail on a pole in the garden "as a warning to other woodchucks," much as the heads of traitors were mounted on pikes and displayed on medieval city walls. Hearing such stories, I began to resent the creature as much for what it might do to me as to my garden.

It was now about two weeks since the chuck had made its first appearance, and still I had not seen it or found its den. I had almost decided to invest in a live trap when one day, about noon, I happened to glance out of a window and spotted a brown-gray form at the far end of the garden, by the pole beans. It was a large, squat animal—portly, you might have said— and was waddling leisurely down the bean row, methodically nibbling off the protruding tendrils like a stout old woman in a fur coat carefully pruning her row of house plants.

I did not have time to think. Hours of hard, sweaty work, a considerable investment of time and money, and an irresistible feeling of possessiveness combined with the sight of the creature to galvanize me into action. I leaped out the back door, grabbed the nearest object—my son's baseball bat—raced down the slope to the garden, vaulted the fence, and confronted the woodchuck face to face, brandishing my weapon, full of primitive, unthinking vengeance.

I had rushed the animal so that it would not have time to climb back out, but I need not have worried. It did not seem to notice me at all until I was beside it. Then it turned and looked at me, not with alarm, but with a nearsighted, perplexed air. It pressed up against the fence, beneath the bean frame, and then finally turned and faced me with that impersonal defiance all cornered wild animals seem to possess. I had time to notice that one of its upper incisors was broken off before I brought down the bat.

It died hard, "the sign of a primitive mammal," I have been told. All I know is that it took several blows directly on the head before it finally lay still, its skull smashed, dark blood staining the mulch hay and the green leaves of the pole beans. I remember resenting it even as I swung the bat for not dying more quickly, for forcing me to continue on in what I had not wanted to do until it was done. And when it was over, I stood there, shaking, full of the realization that I had just taken warm-blooded life in the most brutal fashion in the middle of that sunlit backyard garden.

After a minute or two I prodded the dead woodchuck with the bat, turning it over, and saw eight distended teats on its underside, four on the upper chest and four on the lower belly. So I had killed a mother as well—would I have done it anyway if I had known that? I found myself torn between wondering about the fate of its young, born blind, and hoping they were not old enough to fend for themselves.

I went to the house to get a pair of gloves and, returning, carried the body out of the garden and under some trees. It was heavy, weighing more than ten pounds, I guessed. I examined it in the shade, trying to learn something from it or think of some use for it. The natural history museum might want its skeleton, but the smashed skull made it useless as a specimen. I thought of skinning it, but its fur—thin, ratty, and infested with ticks—told me only that its life was brutish and unenviable. In *The Joy of Cooking* I found a recipe for woodchuck: "Dress as for rabbit, but watch for and remove 7 to 9 small sacs or kernels in the small of its back and under the forearm." Were these scent glands? I never found out, for despite its fat, vegetable-stuffed stomach, its limbs and body felt scrawny, with little meat on them.

At that point I realized that I had no stomach for further attempts to justify the taking of its life. I had made no pact of use or knowledge with this animal. I was simply trying to find some intellectual context into which to put the act of violence I had committed, one that had repelled me but that I had nonetheless intensely desired. I had eliminated a creature I could not, or was not willing to, deal with in any other way, and that was all.

Let us at least keep the nature of its death honest, I thought. So I picked it up and carried it off some distance into the woods, leaving it there without ceremony for the earth to use as it saw fit. As I came back, the death already began to seem distant, petty, unimportant. And yet, as a distasteful song will at times spring unbidden to the mind, I found a phrase repeating itself perversely in my head, one of those bits of saccharine verse put on small wrought-iron signs decked with birds and flowers, the kind sold as border decorations in gift shops and hardware stores:

> Man is closer to God in a garden
> Than anyplace else on earth.

4

It is April again, and once more I stand just outside the garden gate, feeling the new sun on my back, smelling the raw-earth smell, drawn like the redwings to their marshes and the peepers to their bogs. Yet now I hesitate, weighing the lumpy sack of peas in my palm, looking at the rabbit fencing stretched around the locust-post perimeter, with the finished groundhog fencing buried beneath it.

How can we not hesitate on the brink of such a place? Francis Bacon wrote that "He that hath a wife and children hath given hostages to fortune," but he that hath cabbages and cucumbers may give even more. When I remember previous summers, and particularly the last one, this garden seems to have been an arena more often than a refuge, and I more of a combatant than a husbandman, against an earth that has sometimes seemed capable of an almost active malice. Why go through all this trouble again? I doubt whether I could economically justify the time I put into it, nor can I swear that I am always able to tell the difference between a fresh-picked and a fresh-frozen bean.

Gardening, I have learned, can be good for your health but hard on your equilibrium. No enterprise has so radically changed my easy ideas about wild creatures and my relationship to them. The blood on the bean leaves is gone, but things have been revealed to me about myself that I might rather not have known. How hastily, wrapped in our thin blankets of technological insulation, we have tried to change centuries of ingrained sensibilities with glib phrases like "Our friend, the woodchuck," only to be caught up short by our own capacity for brutality and by the complexities of the simplest relationships out in the open.

This business of gardening is more than I originally bargained for. It has proven to be a mixture of compromise and pain, luck and brutality, and, like life itself, its harvests, except for radishes, are always uncertain.

So I no longer begin in innocence. There is a curious ambivalence in my approach to the garden now, something like the behavior of our local terns when they return at about this time of the year from distant tropical wintering grounds to their nesting colonies along our beaches. Ornithologists have remarked how these birds, upon arriving, seem at once drawn to the breeding site and yet reluctant to "set down." This ambivalent behavior has been interpreted as expressing "a certain amount of hostility to be overcome" toward the nesting site, as though, in the older birds at least, they recognized it as a place of both fruition and crucifixion.

But then, I have also learned that neither I nor my crops are really so fragile after all, once the false bloom of perfect expectations is off the enterprise. After the violent encounter with the woodchuck, I found that the lettuce, as well as my sensibilities, began slowly to heal. The bush beans and peas, too, came back in a sea of new blossoms. The pole beans, replanted, rose again and twined up the stringed frame like a green harp. The potatoes, sprouting green volcanoes out of their hills, survived their bugs and cooked all summer in their underground ovens, spilling into our clam buckets in the fall. And the tomatoes, as usual, inundated us at last in a red flood.

Even the corn, always the most uncertain and troublesome of all my crops, came to an unexpected harvest at the end of that woodchuck summer. Normally, the cornstalks that survive early browsing by deer and subsequent borer infestations are lost to raccoons and squirrels.

It is uncanny how these creatures know just when the ears are ripe. Each year, in mid-August, usually on the morning of the day I plan to pick them, I come out to find the stalks bent and fallen across one another, as though blown down by a windstorm. Ears are strewn everywhere, husks pulled back, with three or four rows of kernels eaten on each one and then discarded. All in all, it hardly seems worth the trouble of setting off room for this crop, but I usually put in at least a small patch, if only to see the ripe, golden tassels waving proudly on seven-foot stalks for a few weeks in the summer sun.

That year the corn suffered its usual mid-August devastation, but at about the same time I came upon a letter in a gardening magazine that suggested putting a radio among the corn rows at night to scare away predators. It sounded so improbable that I decided to give it a try. Propping up my remaining stalks, I placed my portable Sony under a box in the middle of the patch and left it, like some garrulous sentry, to guard what was left.

Much to my surprise, it worked. What ears had survived the initial assault came to fruition under that sonic umbrella. One night, just before going to bed, I went out into the garden to turn on the radio. There had been a thunderstorm that afternoon and the garden was flooded with moonlight, puddles, and mist. I stood, barefoot in my pajama bottoms, among the tall, treelike stalks, the long, wet, curved leaf fronds, and the burgeoning, milky, husk-shrouded ears, while down among the ribbed bases of the corn the bland, reassuring voice of CBS News saturated my toes with stories of repression in El Salvador and Poland—and discouraged squirrels.

So now in April the earth has come round once more, and I know why I pause here at the gate, holding the sack of seed peas like a young girl clutching her purse at the edge of a dance floor. It is not her first time there. She has learned many of the steps and danced with many partners, and she may even guess with whom she will move across the bright, polished floor tonight.

Yet she pauses briefly, not from doubt or misgivings, but from the knowledge that she has gleamed at previous dances and that precedes her out onto the floor. For she knows that in order to fully participate in the sweep and joy of its rhythms, the outcome of that generative and insistent music must be forever past knowing, open to events and influences beyond her control or even anticipation.

And so at last I go in through the gate, kneel down to the unspoken earth, and begin once more putting in the seed.

CHAPTER 5

Roads

1

The road I live on is not very old, as roads go here. It shows up on town maps a hundred-years old, but not on others two-hundred-years old—which dates it broadly. And yet it is one of the oldest dirt roads left in Brewster, and one of the few unpaved town-owned roads remaining at all.

About eight-tenths of a mile long, the road runs in a winding, meandering course from nowhere in particular to nowhere in particular, which probably accounts for its still-unpaved state. For a good part of its route, steep, rock-strewn hills converge downward to the road on both sides, suggesting that its present layout may have been determined by a rift in the glacial moraine, twisting and turning like a dry river valley toward Cape Cod Bay. An old, abandoned farmhouse, said to have been the first dwelling in the area, still stands on a small, grassy rise midway along its length and may have called the road into existence originally. Its official name, Red Top Road, derives from the same vanished Methodist meetinghouse that gave its name to the cemetery next door to my house. At present it has six occupied houses, five of which—including mine—were built within the last ten years.

Because it is a dirt road of minor importance, Red Top Road is not so scrupulously or so frequently cleaned and scraped as other public roads in the town. As a result, the life of the bordering oak woods encroaches upon it more readily. The roadside wildflowers are richer and more numerous, from April mayflowers to late-November asters. In summer, ant hills and the burrows of digger wasps sprout over its soft, yielding surface. Occasionally, a daring shrub or pitch-pine seedling will try to take root in the roadbed itself.

The dirt embankments, roughcut out of the stony hillsides and higher than my head in places, hold a wealth of lichens and mosses, woven together in rich, subtle, broken tapestries of greens and golds. These shoulders contain numerous holes and burrows, the homes of mice, chipmunks, voles, snakes, and other small creatures whose tracks I find running from side to side across the road after a winter snowfall. Even in summer its surface is dusty enough to record the various overlapping travels of horses, cars, men, pheasants, dogs, raccoons, foxes, skunks, and others who use it. Thus it keeps its own statistics and takes its censuses throughout the year, though they have never made it into the official town reports.

The road itself changes character with the seasons. In summer it is soft and cushiony underfoot, cool shaded and silent. In winter it becomes as hard as any highway, unyielding and open to the sky, so that when I stamp my foot the vibrations echo up into the iron hills. In March, however, when rains pour down on its unthawed surface, it can become an unwalkable and undrivable quagmire in places, reminding me that, like any road, paved or not, its existence is to some extent artificially maintained. Because it is a town way, it is plowed after snowstorms (though it is generally last on the list and our ephemeral Cape snowfalls have usually melted by themselves before the plow trucks arrive), and twice a year the ruts and potholes are graded smooth.

If it did not receive this minimal municipal servicing, even I might find it inconvenient to live on. Yet I love all of its various surfaces and responses to the seasons, conditions that invite and support small mysteries and surprising dramas the year round. On my walks I catch glimpses of deer moving up the bordering slopes like warm, brown curtains behind the winter maze of gray trunks, a grouse taking a sand bath in the middle of the road, a woodcock darting into the underbrush, salamanders or turtles migrating toward their breeding sites, a broad-winged hawk pouncing on a chipmunk, and, once or twice, a fox.

In late fall and early winter, the roadsides afford me an excellent opportunity to examine the deserted nests of last summer's birds. These nests, invisible all summer, now stand out like hairy coconuts in the leafless shrubs or the crotches of trees, and I like to try to guess the identity of their departed residents from the structure and materials used: the wide, bulky nests of catbirds, usually placed in thick catbrier or viburnum thickets; the more delicate, cup-shaped nests of song sparrows and yellow warblers, constructed entirely of grasses or wiry rootlets and set low to the ground: grackle and robin nests, characterized by their middle layer of mud sandwiched between leaves and grasses, and usually placed in spruce or other ever-green branches.

Not all of these nests are deserted, however. In the fall many are recycled by rodent families for winter shelters. Often the mice fashion a roof over the nest with rootlets or strips of cedar bark and gnaw a small hole in the side for an entrance. One October day I spotted what looked like a small, flattened, furry, quivering creature lying just beyond our driveway in the middle of the dirt road. On closer inspection it turned out to be the remains of a nest that had been built in an overhanging oak branch some fifteen feet above the road. Lifting its edge carefully, I discovered a family of white-footed mice, two brown adults and four small, dark gray young, cowering and trembling and staring at me with black, shiny, panicked eyes as though I were judgment itself. They seemed unhurt by their fall but made no attempt to flee. Possibly, I thought, they were traumatized by what for them must have been the equivalent of a major earthquake. On the other hand, what is the life of a mouse but one continuous trauma, from hasty birth to violent death? I got a shovel from the house and lifted them, nest and all, over to the roadside.

Even from a car, I am more likely to see wildlife along this road than on most others, for it is not yet so wide or so traveled that it cuts off all other arteries of passage. I have never found an animal killed by a car on Red Top, though it has its share of deaths and injuries. The difference is that instead of the anonymous smears of animal life that pave our faster and more lethal highways, the shapes I encounter here—the stiff form of a frozen kinglet, or an ill-timed butterfly—are usually left whole for me to interpret as best I might.

One day last fall my neighbor Pete Wanderlich stopped by the house holding a dead snowy egret upside down by its feet. Dangling there, it looked much smaller than the live egrets I had observed out in our local marshes, more like an elongated rooster. But even in death it was a beautiful and brightly painted bird with a snowy white body some twenty inches long from head to tail, long, thin mud-colored legs, and yellow enameled toes. The bill was nearly six inches long, horizontally flattened, with naked yellow skin at the base. And the eyes—those round, glaring heron eyes that in life had reflected and encased their watery prey—still seemed to stare at me with a fixed determination.

I took the egret from Pete's hand and held it by its legs. Despite the eyes, it felt more lifeless than most dead birds. The slender, S-shaped neck hung limply down like an encased stalk of cracked spaghetti. The force that had once moved and drawn together this gangly, strung-out assembly of limbs and extremities into a form of surpassing grace and ability had absconded, leaving me holding a feathered bag of nerves and bones, a marionette whose strings had been cut.

But cut by what? This road is an unlikely place to find an egret, a bird of salt marshes and barrier beaches, alive or dead. I had never before seen one within a mile of our house. Pete said that he had first spotted it the previous evening while driving along Red Top in his pickup. It lay by the roadside, and standing over it was another large bird, too obscure to identify in the gathering dusk, which flew off at his approach. He did not stop then, but the next day, on his way to work, he saw the egret still lying there, white in the morning sun.

I spread out the egret's wings and marveled at the incredibly pure whiteness of its underplumage. The only marks on its body were a deep puncture wound on the breast just under the right wing, heavily staining the underside of the primaries with broad rose splotches, and a smaller, bloodless puncture on the right shoulder.

What was this marsh stalker doing dead on a dirt road in the middle of an oak forest high in the morainal hills? It seemed unlikely that it had been shot. The most probable scenario was that the second bird had been a hawk or an owl (an owl, most likely, given the time of day) which had taken the egret in midflight over the Cape and was preparing to eat it when my neighbor came along in his truck, scaring it off. There was no way to prove my hypothesis, of course, but at least it explained the egret's presence and the deep puncture wounds. Still, if the bird had been taken by an owl, why hadn't it returned to the carcass during the night?

This road, however, is only a small part of an earth littered with the final acts of natural tragedies, and rarely do we have even this much with which to reconstruct the course of events and the character of the participants.

2

About half a mile down Red Top Road from my house stands the old Black family homestead, a ramshackle one-and-a-half-story farmhouse—tiny even by Cape standards—abandoned for decades and fast falling apart. Not only most of the shingles but much of the flooring is gone. The north wall has come loose from the sills and flaps in the raw spring winds. The narrow brick chimney has been lopped off below the roof line and boarded over, and a series of attached, tin-roofed sheds trails off sadly behind the house. To the southwest of this motley collection of decaying buildings, the land drops down into a meandering, brier-barricaded maple swamp, and beyond the swamp it rises again into a hillside scarred with the looming roads and cul-de-sacs of Red Top's first housing development.

Staring out the vacant front gable window of the old house is a black-and-white cat, the only resident these days, keeping out even the barn swallows. Yet not long ago this was a place of life and work, and the children of people born and raised here still live nearby. Though it is derelict now, its gradual decay, its piecemeal shredding by the wind and the years, has given it a certain grace and fitness, as though, like some of the old, rotting locust trunks behind it, it too were an organic part of the landscape. In fact, however, the property is officially part of the new development beyond the swamp. An incongruous white real-estate sign is nailed above the window where the cat sits, signifying that the building's ultimate fate is likely to be not gradual decay but quick obliteration in the face of yet another marching subdivision.

In a small, grassy field just north of the old farmhouse, another kind of march is in progress. Here an army of young, spindly locust saplings is rapidly invading the field, their slim trunks still smooth and speckled and dotted with sharp, dark thorns. Abandoned fields on the Cape seem to be reclaimed primarily by pitch pines, red cedars, or black locusts, depending on soil and moisture conditions. Locusts seem to do best on poorer, wetter inland sites, for they are nitrogen-fixers, enriching the soil they grow in.

All three pioneer species are hardy and fast growing, but unlike the evergreens, the black locust spreads primarily by root suckers rather than by seeds. A locust's root system is shallow but extensive, and one tree may send up a shoot as far as twenty feet away. If I were carefully to scrape the soil from the surface of this field, I would reveal a continuous network of roots, a literal family tree.

Behind the house, at the back edge of the field where an old stone boundary wall runs, are the brittle, rotting forms of the patriarchal locusts from which these younger trees have advanced. Many of the huge, deeply furrowed trunks have fallen over on one another, or cracked off halfway up. Yet they maintain a tenacious hold on life, sprouting new shoots from the lower limbs or sending up a series of auxiliary trunks along their prostrate spines.

In winter nothing is quite so spectral in appearance as the bare, silhouetted forms of these old trees, catching cold fire in their top branches from the setting sun. But in late spring the locusts enjoy a striking, if brief, moment of glory. They lift their long, crooked limbs high into the air, where their light, feathery leaves wave in the slightest breeze. There, up in the arching branches, the beautiful locust flowers begin to appear: large, soft, pendulous clusters of white, fragrant blossoms, the showiest of all our uncultivated trees.

There is something arresting, even mystical, about these tortured, elongated shapes spiked with thorns, now flowing with such sweet, drooping abundance. They also seem, in their lean crookedness, appropriate to our spare landscape, though black locusts are not native to this part of New England. Botanists believe that the tree originally grew only as far north as Pennsylvania, but it arrived on Cape Cod well over 150 years ago and is now widespread through the fifteen towns. Perhaps the wrecked hulks at the back of the field were planted not long after the sills of the crumbling farmstead were first laid.

One June morning I stood inside the old house, examining its ruins, though I did not expect to find much. As an acquaintance of mine who studies these old places put it, "The people who lived here didn't have much and didn't leave much." But I had not come to find artifacts so much as to try to drink in the depths of its commonplace and unrecorded history, to touch and read the mute signs of a long and varied life now fast coming to a close.

Where the south wall once stood is a gaping hole that lets in the morning light. The original hearth is boarded over and the fireplace converted to a stove flue, though a small wooden mantel remains. To the left of the chimney is a wooden cupboard, its open shelves still backed with a flower-patterned wallpaper, now faded and curled. On the right side is a small alcove where the stove apparently stood, for the low ceiling above is blackened with soot from years of close, unvented cooking. A remarkable amount of plaster, of the old horsehair and clamshell variety, is still intact on the ceiling and remaining walls, and in places sets of multiplication tables have been scrawled in pencil. An application for the Coast Guard, dated 1909, was once found inside one of the walls, and another time some teenagers dug up a yellowed skull from beneath the floorboards, creating a stir of excitement until it was identified as that of a pig. I did make one find myself that morning: under a set of narrow and incredibly steep stairs that runs behind the chimney up to a small sleeping room, I uncovered an old mouse nest, also long abandoned, made from the shredded pages of a 1952 *Boston Herald*.

As I poked around that old wreck of a house, I heard a noise outside that sounded something like a muffled telephone bell, followed by the creaking of a gigantic door. Stepping outside through the open wall, I looked up and saw a flicker hard at work among the high branches and white flower clusters of one of the large locusts just beside the house. As he worked his way down the trunk, pecking away, the sound of his drumming had not only a definite pitch but one that changed several times as he descended. The woodpecker made the iron heartwood of that old tree sing, and as he did I noticed something even more curious: out of the clefts and scars of the still-living locust were growing several other tree species, including a two-foot-high cedar sapling and a young cherry tree nearly four inches in diameter.

I walked down off the small rise and away from the house to the locust grove at the back of the field. There, at my feet, I found a large box turtle, poised motionless in the lush, dark green grass that grew beneath the trees. The grass was wet from rain that had fallen the night before, and the turtle's shell glistened, its intricate yellow markings standing out brightly, like the patterns of animal tracks. As I picked him up, he quickly withdrew his head, hissing sharply as he collapsed his lungs to make room in the shell for the rest of him. He peered out at me with deep, bright-red, reptilian eyes between triple slits of shell, folds of gray skin and pale, upsliding lids. He seemed so to fit in this place of slow, deeply mingled human and natural history. Rain, locust blossoms, an old house, lush new grass, and a turtle. How easy it is to be engulfed by such simple matrices of commonplace things! Yet the apparently casual forces that brought these elements here together on an ordinary June morning are essential and irrepressible, despite real-estate signs and encroaching roads. I felt things in the making here, plans afoot, and developments as yet untried, unfolding in the sweet air above me.

3
———

On a hot morning in early July, I took a walk down Red Top to the new housing development, whose paved entrance lies beyond the old Black place, at the far end of the road. This development is one of the last of the old small-lot "spec developments" in Brewster, large, grid-type subdivisions that spread themselves over the Cape landscape during the building boom of the 1960s and early 1970s. After the economic recession of 1973, most of these latter-day projects "died on the vine," as the saying goes, leaving in many cases mazes of rough, uncompleted roads spread upon the land.

Although the half a mile or so of roads in this development have recently been asphalted and new utility poles line their shoulders, the poles are still wireless and the lots stand empty and unsold. That morning the only inhabitant was a large, yellow, nasty-looking dog that stood at the entrance as though guarding it. He glared at me as I approached and gave a low growl, but slinked off to one side and let me pass in.

This development at least makes no pretensions to Cape Cod quaintness, either by calling itself a "village" or by naming its streets after fictitious sea captains. Rather, it possesses a certain straightforward ugliness and candor of purpose. The names of the subdivision and of its roads come right out of Boston, reflecting the urban money that put them there, although most of the street signs and even some of their metal poles have been broken off and pulled down by vandals.

The roads appear to have been laid out with a geometric unconcern for topography, plastered upon the landscape with cut-and-fill construction to accommodate the maximal number of lots. The initial result of this method was a scene of barren, eroding hillsides, but nature has done much in only a few years to cloak and heal the scars. On this summer's day the untended roadsides sported crowds of oxeye daisies, fleabane, red clover, and cypress spurge, all in bright flower. From a young stand of pitch pine colonizing a stripped embankment, I heard a hidden prairie warbler trilling out its ascending chromatic song. At one intersection marked by a beheaded street-sign pole, a particularly barren stretch of gravelly fill spread out under the hot sun, with only a few wiry patches of grass dotting its scraped expanse. Even the alien weeds had not made much progress here, but in the very middle of this miniature desert I found several soft, gray-green tufts of native poverty grass, cupping their lovely, diminutive yellow blossoms.

The main subdivision road lurches down toward Round Pond, an exquisite small kettle-hole pond hidden from sight by a bowl of surrounding hills. Where the road skirts its edge the surveyor's plans show a "community beach," that obligatory amenity of all developments possessing anything larger than a mud puddle within their bounds. In this case the "beach" is a purely abstract designation, consisting of a steep, eroded bluff that drops some fifteen feet directly into the pond. With some difficulty I made my way down the washed-out banks and stood at last at the bottom, in three inches of water, while on either side of me dozens of green frogs shrieked and jumped into the water, plopping in succession like small, green waves breaking along the shore.

As I turned to climb back up the bank, I saw the yellow dog, who must have followed me, peering down over the edge of the bluff with a menacing look. Sensing that he was a coward at heart, I picked up a stone and clambered to the top. Again he stepped aside, but as I went on along the roads, he continued to skulk behind, disappearing now and then behind the pines, but always showing up again just when I thought he had left for good.

Already portions of the pavement on these poorly constructed roads were caving in, producing small potholes and broken trenches. Shattered glass and a few old tires littered the streets, heightening the urban effect. At a turnaround on one of the dead-end streets, I found signs of a recent unauthorized party, apparently innocent enough and even calorie conscious, in the form of a dozen or so cans and bottles of Diet Pepsi. I came to the end of another cul-de-sac, which bordered the maple swamp that stretched north toward the old Black house. Here, just off into the woods, I found the remains of a campfire, the only other sign of human occupation along the black maze of unused roads. The fire had a poignant, forlorn look about it, as though it might have belonged to the ghost of some old Indian who had climbed up out of the swamp mists, taken a brief, sad glance around, and then disappeared down the embankment again.

I sat down in the shade of the oaks next to the dead campfire and tried to come to grips with the mixture of strong feelings that such scenes always generate within me: anger and disgust at the scarred hillsides and clumsy roads, which proclaimed such blatant indifference to all natural fitness and proportion; reassurance and comfort in nature's slow healing of such carelessly inflicted wounds; guarded delight in the project's current state of failure—guarded because I know that all such victories of neglect are at best temporary here. I know, for instance, that this particular development is now in the hands of its third broker, one whose sales force is billed as "aggressive and professional." Lately the number of building permits in the town has begun to rise again, and it seems only a matter of time before the yellow dog will have plenty of company.

I do not enjoy such feelings, which seem to force me to take sides against my own kind and to wish failure on their enterprises. They strike me as unhealthy and unnatural sentiments, for surely there is something bold and daring about our race that we should rightfully admire and cherish. Perhaps, as some charge, a conservationist outlook breeds misanthropy, but I don't think so. If there is any perversity, it seems to lie in the nature of such projects as this, which distort and degrade the notion of "enterprise."

Most land speculators seem to have forgotten the meaning of their profession, if they ever knew it. The early homesteaders were at least speculators in the true sense, not men who believed that an investment of cash ought to guarantee success. Life was then, like the Republic itself, a proposition still to be tested, sometimes in war, but more often in the simple, daily tasks of making a living. To speculate then meant to guess the weather, the cranberry harvest, the scallop crop, the flounder runs, the rain, and the frost. Whether setting out seed or fish traps, one put one's knowledge of land and sea on the line, risking disaster to secure the basic necessities of life.

These roads, on the other hand, were bulldozed in and paved over, not because homesites were in demand at the time, but because the undersized lots (one-third the area now required by local zoning laws) would otherwise have been rescinded and the developers forced to come in with larger and fewer lots. The whole place, in other words, was built backward, not in response to any genuine human need, but in an attempt to create a demand for itself, asking the world to pave a path to its door. It rode the tide of an earlier building boom and now lies momentarily stranded in limbo, neither developed nor undeveloped, a blank on the landscape.

But modern real-estate economics demand that no place like this can be allowed to fail gracefully, to fall softly back into nature. An irreversible investment has been made here. The land has been claimed for all time—surveyed, set, and land courted—and no relinquishment is possible. Though weeds grow in and wildflowers thrive, though potholes form and sands blow across its cracked asphalt roads, it will never be abandoned for good. If necessary, it will be resold, refinanced, and rebrokered until doomsday, until its abstract destiny, imposed by abstract entities for abstract profits, has one day been realized, whether anyone—those who live near it, those who finance it, those who sell it, or even those who finally live here— genuinely desires it or not. . . .

My thoughts, I realized, were becoming increasingly blurry, like the cracked and twisted landscape before me, which had grown hazy in the waves of the midday heat rising from the pavement. As I looked out through the trees, the yellow hound emerged into view again, turning a corner and lumbering down the street in my direction, still dogging me from a safe, but constant, distance. He would do so until I left. And so, rather than retrace my steps across the baking, glass-littered streets, I slipped down the embankment off the cul-de-sac and followed my imaginary Indian into the swamp.

CHAPTER 6

Punkhorn

The houses are gone, the little shops are gone,
squirrels preach in the chapel. A row of stone
all now that's left of the cobbler's, or in tall grass
a scrap of harness where once the tannery was.
And the blue lilacs, the grey laylocks, take possession
round every haunted cellar-hole, like an obsession . . .

—CONRAD AIKEN, "Mayflower"

1

When I bought the piece of land on which I built my house, I chose it primarily because it sat in the middle of what appeared to be unspoiled woodland, with a good chance of staying that way for some time. Its trees, largely oak, were the sign of a relatively mature forest, though I later identified thirteen different species of trees within its boundaries, including a couple of wild apple trees and a nice stand of tupelo, or black gum, on the front slope.

The first time I walked the bounds, a brilliant day in early spring, a large grouse the color of the forest floor exploded out of last year's leaves directly in front of me. Along the stone wall that forms the back boundary, I found a green-and-gold garter snake soaking up the April sun on an old lichen-spotted boulder. They appeared to me as signs of the place's wild, abiding nature. It seemed like a desirable neighborhood.

The grouse and the snake did not mislead me, but in the several years I have lived here now, I have gradually come to realize that, despite the landscape's wild aspect, there is hardly a square foot of ground in the immediate vicinity that does not bear, directly or indirectly, marks of the past hand of man.

I knew before I ever came here, of course, that the old life and most of the Cape Codders who lived it were long gone. But the impression they made went deeper than I first thought, beyond an old road like Red Top or a few obvious relics like the old Black place or the gravestones next door. Since moving in, I have found that various signs of these past lives, unnoticed at first, continually surface, like the buried rocks in my garden that seem to work their way up afresh each winter, giving me unexpected jolts when I start to turn the soil over in the spring.

These oak woods, for instance, which from my yard seem to stretch out as far as I can see in an unbroken expanse, are actually crisscrossed with a woven pattern of old wagon roads, cart tracks, and footpaths. Some are still quite traversable. My neighbor's driveway follows one wood road, my own another. Others, long abandoned, are lost to sight, often indiscernible even on close inspection. These are revealed only on certain winter days when a light snowfall and the slant of winter light trace and illuminate their forgotten routes like faint white lines of memory.

Today a few of these old byways are still kept open by hunters, joggers, horses, dog walkers, and meanderers like myself who roam these woods for their own sake. But in the past, I sense, they formed a more intimate, if slower, network of human communication than we have today. Men walked to see their neighbors, to carry water, to go blueberrying at Round Pond, to get their hair cut at the neighborhood barbershop, to attend services at Red Top Meetinghouse. Their feet wore an intricate pattern of trails through these hills, which today look not very different from the still narrower game trails one finds running off through the huckleberry and the bracken fern.

In an age before designated street names, some of these old roads and footpaths gradually acquired identities, evocative of the related neighborliness of the past. Red Top Road itself used to be known as Nate's Road, for Nathan Black, its sole resident for many years. From the top of the low ridge west of Red Top a narrow trail winds down to the road, a footpath still locally known as Aunt Thankful's Path, though no one in the area is sure who Aunt Thankful was or where she lived.

Running beneath the same canopy of oak and beech, and intersecting these paths and wood roads, are the more regular lines of low stone walls, built of rounded glacial boulders. Most of the stones are typical of this section of the moraine: large hernia makers that were dragged and rolled into place by men and oxen. The walls are broken in many places now, pulled down by gravity on some of the steeper slopes, or where a new subdivision road has been put through. Many of the stones now lie nearly buried with leaf mold, pine needles, and lichen. But they nevertheless represent the first totally abstract lines made upon the face of this landscape. Unlike the roads and paths, whose courses were in large part governed by the contours of the hills, the stone walls follow deeded boundary lines. Where the walls turn a corner, one can often find an old squared granite post, with "NB" or "JH" carved in it, or in a later version, old galvanized well points stuck in the ground with the owners' initials painted on them. Today the boundaries as well as the owners have changed in many places, but the walls continue to mark the old limits, arcing steeply down into the kettle holes and leaping back up the slopes, massive and heavy, like saurian vertebrae.

By the side of the wood roads, I frequently come on old bottle dumps, testaments to the casual disposal methods practiced by the former inhabitants, and sometimes mute evidence of the tenor of their lives here. In this land of geologic youth, the artifacts in these dumps strike me with the force of fossils, and must serve as such since the Cape can claim no real ones. There are heaps of broken crockery and plates, rusted pots and coal scuttles, pieces of broken farm implements, and lots of square, green-tinted bottles. These last are usually either medicine bottles—queer old panaceas and tonics of the age, whose curious names are spelled out in raised glass letters: "Mrs. Harvey's Cherry Elixir," "Beef, Wine & Iron"—or else broken whiskey flasks. Life wears out, these dumps seem to say, and people with them.

Just west of our house, below the rim of Berry's Hole, is a fairly large dump of this sort, containing parts of old stoves and water heaters as well as lesser debris, all discarded from an old house that once stood a few yards back from the edge. One day in early summer I was poking around this old dump when I became aware of small lavender petals falling to the ground all about me. When I scanned the woods to see what shrub or bush they might have come from, I noticed that the oak trunks were wound and cabled tightly with long, thick vines, some over two inches in diameter. The vines wound their way up into the forest canopy some twenty-five feet overhead, where, like exotic orchids blooming in some tropical forest, they burst out in masses of large, purple, pealike flowers that hung down in drooping clusters. It was the first time I had ever seen wisteria in the woods, and it was strange to think of these fragrant adornments of old Cape homesteads grown to monstrous wild form here in the dark shade of the oaks.

The inhabitants of the vanished house from which these vines had escaped were casual by repute. The rumor of an old murder lingered about the site, and the house itself had been dismantled over a decade ago. Now only a large old apple tree, the dump, and the escaped wisteria vines remain—a legacy of trash and blossoms.

Other wild apple trees that I have found here and there in the woods testify to the former existence of orchards, and an old sand and gravel pit about a quarter mile from my house is still known by older residents as "the turnip field." The oaks themselves, for that matter, are hardly original cover, but rather the hardy survivors of repeated cuttings and chronic wildfires in the past, leaving these stunted, commercially worthless oak monocultures, which today remain equally vulnerable to chainsaws, bulldozers, and the cyclical infestations of the gypsy moth, another human import.

Even the topography of these hills has been changed by human enterprise, though in ways not always evident at first. Dozens of small swamps in the neighborhood, which now grow thick with maple and cedar saplings, were all working cranberry bogs two or three generations ago. Around the perimeter of almost every one of these abandoned bogs I can find at least one large gouge in the hillside, sometimes twenty or thirty feet across. These gouges once served as sand pits for the bogs. Most of these pits are now lined with huckleberry, sheep laurel, bearberry, and young pitch pines. They are a good place to look for fox burrows, which are often dug into the soft sand at the top of the bank just below the binding layer of sod and tree roots.

The landscape, the "neighborhood," seen in this way, becomes after a while a curious mixture of past and present, of man-made and earth-made. In a way, the archaeologist and the ecologist have similar points of view, for both see all of the earth's various features attached to one another at some point, either in space or time. Here, I came to see, the local ghosts had not been dispossessed but rather absorbed and transformed by the land, which itself had been changed in the process. Each was something different from what it had been before the other came and possessed it. Man had not passed from the scene here, but into it.

2

Lillian Scott lives at the top of a hill on Stony Brook Road in the house where she was born nearly eighty years ago. She is the daughter of Frank Ellis, who once owned most of the land west of my house, including Berry's Hole and a good deal of the surrounding hills. Her house is a characteristic, though not common, type of Cape Cod architecture: a small two-story building with a glassed-in front porch that seems just big enough to house her ample, friendly body and a feisty little white poodle that is her only companion.

Her late husband, Jim Scott, was an engineer who worked outside Boston for many years. When he retired, they bought a home in Florida, spending the winters there and returning to Cape Cod in the summer. After Jim's death Lillian continued to go south for a few winters, but she finally decided that "it was too much trouble" and sold the Florida property. Now she lives year round again in the house where she grew up.

With no close family nearby, Lillian, like many widows, spends much of her day watching soap operas on TV. In nicer weather she is often outside tending her colorful flower garden. To one side of the house is a partial rock foundation that was once the site of her father's barn. The sloping field behind the house was a pasture when she was young. A young man who grew up nearby remembers sledding in the field as a boy. Now it is fairly grown over to red cedar and black locust.

Those of us who live in the neighborhood look in on Lillian now and then in order to shovel a path through the snow to her mailbox, cut her grass, or simply visit. She is always glad to have company, and whenever I drop in she leaves the TV on as we talk, as one might leave on the lights. Her house is, like herself, friendly and comfortable. Her poodle, like most bantam barkers, is overly affectionate at close range, and her talk is punctuated with ineffectual, perfunctory admonitions hurled in its direction—"Chinny, stop it." "Chinny, what is the matter with you?"—as if she were brushing at flies.

With "The Young and the Restless" panting heavily in the background, Lillian Scott tells me about the neighborhood as it was when she was a girl.

For as long as she can remember, this section of West Brewster has been known as "Punkhorn." She doesn't know why. It is a local term that seems to have been applied indiscriminately to several areas on the Cape. As used by people in other parts of town to refer to our neighborhood, however, the name has traditionally carried subtle connotations of deprecation and ridicule, a sense, as near as I can gather, of being "out in the sticks."

As a child attending the district school, she used to be embarrassed when she and her friends were called "Punkhorners," and they never referred to themselves as such. Later, when she went to the town's first centralized high school (now the Brewster Plastics Factory), there were, she recalls, neighborhood gangs of boys that frequently got into fights after classes or at socials. The "Punkhorn gang" always seemed to be involved in more than its share of scraps.

Punkhorners, young and old, have for some reason always been regarded as "strange" or "different" by the rest of the town. It may have originated with the fact that the Methodists, who built their first meetinghouse in Brewster in Red Top Cemetery, were always regarded as a radical and suspect sect on the Cape.

For years the only black family in town lived at the top of the ridge east of Red Top Road in a one-room house whose fallen-in remains are now hidden by a curtain of locusts and lilacs. Their name was Cassius, or Cash, and stories about them are still told locally, though I have never heard any from native

Punkhorners like Lillian. They appear to have accepted the Cashes as neighbors, though none of the family are buried in the cemetery next door.

George Cassius, the father, was said to have been "not quite right in the head"; he was frequently hauled in by the town constable for vagrancy and other small misdemeanors. A man who knew George in his later years, back in the late 1940s, told me that he was once found wandering around in the restricted area of Camp Edwards Army Base in Falmouth. He was brought before the local judge, who said to him in a patronizing tone, "George, they say you're a bit tetched."

In a high, sing-song voice George replied, "Yew tew, jedge, yew tew!"

A woman from Orleans told me about a white Punkhorn woman whose husband was frequently away from home. "She got pregnant, and when the baby came it was coffee colored. They showed it to her, and she said, 'Well, Doc, you know I have been feelin' kinda poorly lately.' Of course we all knew who the father was."

Punkhorn's eccentric reputation was reinforced in the 1930s and early 1940s when a number of "artist types," writers and painters mostly, bought summer homes in the neighborhood. Even the tolerant Punkhorners began to feel uneasy about this trend. During World War II, George Alexander, who lived down Stony Brook Road toward the herring run, decided to sell his house, a fine, old full Cape. One day he was visited by one of the actresses playing summer stock at the Cape Playhouse in Dennis, a few miles away.

"I hear this house is for sale," she said.

George Alexander looked over the woman's tall, statuesque figure, her long, dark, flowing hair, impeccably applied makeup, low-cut blouse, tight-fitting skirt, sheer nylons, and high-heeled shoes. "Not to your kind it's not," he said, and shut the door.

The spurned actress left and later bought a house in East Dennis, where they weren't so particular about their neighbors. Her name was Gertrude Lawrence.

One of the most successful and permanent artistic immigrants was the poet Conrad Aiken. In 1940 he and his wife, the artist Mary Hoover, bought the old Clark homestead on Stony Brook Road, a short distance east of Red Top Cemetery. It is a vintage, rambling, seventeenth-century saltbox farmhouse that Aiken, with a flair for the literal, baptized "41 Doors." For over thirty summers and nearly that many winters, Conrad Aiken lived at 41 Doors, where he peopled and storied the neighborhood with his dreams, his poems, and his marvelous letters.

Here, for instance, in a letter to his friend Edward Burra, is his description of the Punkhorn neighborhood shortly after their moving in, in September 1940:

"Dear Ed: . . . It really is a lovely place. The country is as simpatico as any I've seen—rolling, wooded, with cleared patches, and far views to the sea, marshy as it approaches sea level, then fine broad sand beaches. Fishing weirs far out, far glimpses of Provincetown. Pines, oaks, deer, and wildlife of every sort—quite alarming. You meet giant wasps in the garden, dragging giant caterpillars by the throat—six foot blacksnakes—woodchucks eating the lettuce—swarms of maggots an inch long trying like salmon to swim up out of the garbage pit—there are times when it seems better to stay indoors! But the whole thing is good. . . . Summer folk have largely gone—our road is very quiet—life is simple. . . ."

Many of Aiken's later poems have a Punkhorn setting, including his long triptych poem "Mayflower," whose central section, one of the loveliest elegies in American poetry, evokes and celebrates the vanished first inhabitants of his house:

. . . Here lies
Mercy or Thankful, here Amanda Clark,
the wife of Rufus; nor do they dread the dark,
but gaily now step down the road past Stony Brook,
call from the pasture as from the pages of a book,
their own book, by their own lives written,
each look and laugh and heartache, nothing forgotten.
Rufus it was who cleared of bullbriar the Long Field,
walled it with fieldstone, and brought to fabulous yield
the clay-damp corner plot, where the wild grape twines.
Amanda planted the cedars, the trumpet-vines,
mint-beds, and matrimony vine, and columbines.
Each child set out and tended his own tree,
to each his name was given. Thus, they still live, still see:
Mercy, Deborah, Thankful, Rufus and Amanda Clark,
trees that praise sunlight, voices that praise the dark.

Yet despite Aiken's eager, imaginative insinuation of himself into the neighborhood and its history, and his genuine affection for the local inhabitants, Punkhorners tended to look on his Bohemian life-style and "artsy" friends with suspicion and referred to him with circumspection as "the po't."

Initially, his only close friend here was Brad Clarke, who, although not a native himself, was a well-liked member of the community and for many years ran the Packet Antiques Shop next to 41 Doors. After the Aikens arrived for the summer, people used to stop in at the shop and ask, "Well, Brad, how's the po't?" In the evenings, I have been told, Brad's mother would regularly pull down all the window shades in the parlor before sitting down. To guests she would explain, "That's so's the po't can't peek in on us."

Nonetheless "the po't" in his later years became not only a literary figure of international stature but eventually also an accepted and even guardedly admired member of the Punkhorn community.

During their years here together, Mary Aiken painted several portraits of her husband. One of the more arresting studies shows him with their Siamese cat Nipperty on his shoulder, while in the background the dark, flowing lineaments of Red Top Graveyard and its crooked gray and white headstones spread out like waves under a fantastic moon.

Conrad Aiken died in 1973 and lies buried in his native city of Savannah, Georgia.

3

Directly across from the old, crumbling Black farmhouse on Red Top Road lives Jennie Baker, née Jennie Black, the daughter and last surviving child of Nathan Black the younger, who died in 1957 at the age of ninety-two. Jennie Black Baker is second cousin to Lillian Scott, and as children they played together in the cemetery while their fathers repaired the white wooden fences and scythed the family plots. She married a local boy, Theron Baker, but now both women live as widows, half a mile apart, in the houses where they were born and raised, divested at last of husbands and other external trappings, returned to home.

Once, in the basement of our elementary school, I came upon an old class picture from 1916 that showed the two of them as young teenagers sitting in adjacent rows at their dark wooden desks, bows in their flat, straight hair. I looked hard at their schoolgirl faces, and it seemed to me that their basic and somewhat divergent outlooks on the world had already formed.

Mrs. Baker is more formal and reserved than her cousin. (Once I referred to her father as Nate, the name by which he was known in life to everyone in the neighborhood. "Nathan," she corrected me, kindly but firmly.) Her house, a dormered Cape built in the last century, is kept neat as a pin, inside and out, though her yard has fewer flowers in it than Lillian's. Instead of a frantic poodle, a quiet black-and-white cat (the one

I had seen in the farmhouse gable window) rests on her lap. And though she turns off the television when visitors come, a flashing row of lights from a CB radio sitting on top of the set lets visitors know she keeps in constant touch with the outside world.

She is very particular about names and dates and knows where everyone in the local graveyard is buried. It was Mrs. Baker, in fact, who until recently was asked to look over any new burial sites in Red Top Cemetery in order to determine whether they contained, as she put it, "any bones without stones." Twelve members of the Black family lie in the cemetery, and four generations of her forebears lived in the tiny farmhouse whose old shell she can see from her front window, rotting away in the locust field across the road.

In 1795 John Harris, "a sea-faring man," and his wife Sarah built a small one-room half-Cape in this remote section of West Brewster, then still part of the neighboring town of Harwich. The Harrises had six children, including a daughter, Elizabeth, who was born in 1803, the year of Brewster's incorporation and one year before her father's death. Elizabeth grew up in the house with her mother and brothers and sisters; in 1822 she married Nathan Black, who came to Punkhorn from South Yarmouth. Nathan and Elizabeth Black continued to live in the house, farming the surrounding land for some forty years and producing ten children. Their son Timothy was born in 1830 and married Bridget Malady, "fresh off the boat from County Cork."

Shortly after the Civil War, Timothy Black built the "new house" across the road, where Mrs. Baker now lives, and moved in with his family. The land for the new house was deeded not to Timothy by his father, Nathan, but to Bridget Black by her mother-in-law, Elizabeth. I asked Mrs. Baker whether this was unusual in those days, but she seemed surprised and even slightly offended by the question. "No, I don't think so," she answered in a clipped tone, and did not elaborate. Perhaps it represented some local tradition of matriarchal descent. At any rate, the Black women have always seemed to end up with their houses.

Jennie Baker's father, Nathan Black the younger, was born to Timothy and Bridget in the old house in 1865. In 1884 he established the Black Hills Emporium, a barbershop, in a small barn in the yard, which he ran for over seventy years. "Nate the Barber," as he was known, was no part-time neighborhood hair chopper, but a real professional, "the only barber in Brewster and Dennis," though he never had any formal training. As a young man, he had helped out in the family's hog-slaughtering business and so may have indirectly picked up the trade from his father, eventually refining it into a tonsorial art. The Emporium boasted two barber chairs ("No Waiting"), though when it got very cold Nate sometimes brought his customers into the house kitchen to trim them. Every Wednesday and Saturday evening, he would put his barbering tools into a satchel and walk two miles over to East Dennis, where he gave shaves and haircuts in the basement of David H. Sears's store. One of the present Brewster selectmen, himself now an elderly man, told me that once when he was a small boy, his father was taking him and his brother over to Nate Black's when they met the barber carrying his satchel along Red Top Road. "He sat us down on a rock and gave us a trim right there."

Besides barbering, Nate Black for many years worked seasonally for Lewis Crowell's cranberry company on Elbow Pond. Mrs. Baker once showed me a picture of her father standing in front of the screening shed by the pond. He looked about thirty, wearing overalls and a wide-brim felt hat, with a long mustache of that era and a tall, lanky frame that seemed made for easy running and long distances.

Mrs. Baker has no more idea than Lillian Scott where the term "Punkhorn" originated, though she also remembers being taunted by it at school. She thinks perhaps it was an old Indian name, or some corruption of one. She is, however, familiar with Aunt Thankful's Path, the old footpath that goes across Red Top Road just north of her house. When she was young, she says, they called it Ikey Dunham's Path, after Ikey Dunham Sears, who lived on the hill west of the road near the old turnip field. In the evenings, Ikey often went to visit the Cashes, who lived on the opposite ridge, by walking down the path, crossing Red Top Road, and climbing the east slope. Ikey was afraid of the dark and, according to Mrs. Baker, was "always hearing strange noises" when he returned home at night. She remembers, as a girl, lying in bed and listening to Ikey pass by, singing in a loud, high, strained voice, "in order to keep things away."

4

One evening in early February, as I was preparing supper in the house, a sudden blast ripped through the air, jarring the glasses on the kitchen shelves. It was quite loud and seemed to come from the direction of Charlie Ellis's shack across the road. There was no aftermath, however, and as it was bitter cold outside, I put it down to a sonic boom and forgot about it.

Charlie himself lives about a mile from his shack in a nineteenth-century farmhouse with an authentic quarter board from the shipwreck *Exminster* nailed up over his barn door. He has been many things during his long life, most recently a lobsterman in Cape Cod Bay. When I first moved here, he was still selling his catch to friends and acquaintances at half the going fish-market price, weighed out on a scale on his front porch. But a few years ago, when he turned eighty, he decided to retire from lobstering and sold most of his gear to his grandson.

Charlie continues to take care of several summer places in the neighborhood, including 41 Doors, which the Aikens bought from Mrs. Ellis's family. Mary Aiken still summers there, and Charlie looks after the place, as he has done for the past forty years. Frequently during the year I see his blue pickup parked in front of 41 Doors as he goes about raking leaves, checking the house after a storm or hard freeze, fixing up the grounds in spring, putting a new roof on one of the outbuildings in summer. He is one of the fixtures there, like the glossy-necked mourning doves that build their fragile nests in the open pitch-pine boughs in the yard each May or like the small brown deer that cross Stony Brook Road in October to feed on the ungathered apples that have fallen in the Aikens' side orchard.

Charlie Ellis's shack sits across from our house on Red Top Road in the middle of an open lot next to a large stand of silverleaf poplars. It is a simple frame building with an extended shed roof in the rear, built of "dimension timber" (precut lumber as opposed to rough boards and beams) and sheathed in a motley of asphalt and wooden sidings. In typical Brewster fashion it is built on the edge of a fairly steep slope, which grows up to sumac each summer, but which Charlie mows down in the fall so that the neighborhood kids can use it for sledding.

As a young man Charlie used the shack as a camp, to hunt the grouse and deer that are still common in the woods around it. More recently it served as a kind of workshop where he repaired his lobster pots and other gear, but the windows were smashed so often by vandals that he was forced to board them all up several years ago. Even so, the shack was broken into last winter and an old potbellied stove, which he had used for nearly fifty years, was stolen.

In spite of this, and the fact that he no longer goes out lobstering, Charlie still visits the shack regularly. I have often walked by the place on crisp winter mornings when a thin plume of blue smoke was rising from the narrow chimney, or on hot, sweltering August afternoons when its windows were all shut up and the door was closed, and heard him tinkering away inside, finding, in the manner of old men, something useful to do in this place of remembered youth.

A few days after the mysterious explosion that rocked our kitchen, I saw Charlie's pickup parked across the road. I walked over to the shack and knocked on the battened door, a little apprehensively, for though I had chatted with Charlie several times, it had always been in the road or outside in the yard. I had never seen the inside of the shack.

He answered my knock promptly and greeted me with that innate courtesy of old country people: "Good morning, Mr. Finch, good morning. Come in, yes, come in."

I entered from bright winter sunshine into the dimly lit darkness of the building's interior. Charlie had installed another old stove to replace the one that had been stolen, and he surprised me by saying that the man who had taken it had sold his property and moved to Maine, so that he didn't expect to get it back.

I said I didn't think the police had found out who had stolen it.

"Oh," he replied, "I have a pretty fair idea who 'twas."

A single bare bulb, hung on a wire from an open ceiling joist, cast a feeble aura into the room where he stood. The walls were mostly uninsulated boards, dark with age. Two smaller side rooms, obscure in the dim light, had once been sleeping rooms but were now stacked with boxes and bed frames.

Charlie offered me a seat in a faded, black-cushioned platform rocker near the stove, sitting himself down on a plain wooden bench across from me. A third person would have had to stand. I asked him whether he had heard the explosion the other day, and he replied, "Oh, that must have been the nitro."

He explained, in a tone he might have used in discussing the weather, that he had been making plans to turn over the shack property to his grandson, "just so's I don't have to worry about it any more." About two weeks before, while cleaning out various items that had accumulated over the decades, he had come upon a large, dusty glass jar on a back shelf that turned out to contain "about a quart and a half" of nitroglycerin. Charlie thought it had probably sat there for at least twenty years, and he had forgotten all about it. In fact, he couldn't even remember what he had bought it for in the first place, but he figured he'd better get rid of it. So he called up Boston and talked to the State Explosives Expert, a man whose sole job, according to Charlie, is to travel around the Commonwealth blowing up and disposing of dangerous materials.

The following week the Expert had come out with the local police chief to Charlie's shack, built a small platform at the bottom of the slope behind it, carefully transported the jar of nitroglycerin down the hill and onto the platform, placed a blasting cap on the jar, strung wires back up the hill and into the shack, and detonated the nitro. The explosion left a hole two feet deep in the ground. That accomplished, the Expert had picked up his equipment and departed, taking with him as a token of appreciation a few of Charlie's old nets and buoys for his suburban house.

"You know," Charlie said to me, "I've been hammering and sawing in here all those years—that stuff might have gone off at any time. Maybe it sounds a bit hard, but it would have served that stove thief right if he'd tried to grab the nitro."

Charlie Ellis is a squat, stocky man with a good deal of that easygoing and impersonal good humor that Melville ascribed to his "Cape Cod man" Stubb, the second mate in *Moby-Dick*. His freckled flesh has sagged somewhat over the years, but he exhibits that quiet stamina of many of the older local natives which seems to come from establishing your pace early and keeping to it. He grew up in an era when, as he says, "living on Cape Cod meant you were poor—though we didn't know we were poor." Still, it was a close life in many ways, close and mean for those of his generation who came after the days of the Cape's merchant-marine glory and before the new tide of tourist dollars. Lacking the open decks of their grandfather's clipper ships or the daily escapes of their grandchildren's TV shows, they often had only themselves and a bleak landscape to confront for long stretches of time. In many of his contemporaries, this bred a dark and sullen introversion, but in Charlie and others of his temperament, it seems to have fostered a kind of readiness to perform, to tell stories and assume roles when they got together or were approached by strangers.

Charlie has told me many stories of his days in the Coast Guard service along the Cape's outer beaches during the years between the two world wars. He served at one time or another, he says, in most of the dozen manned stations that in those days stood fronting the open ocean from Race Point, in Provincetown, to Monomoy Island, south of Chatham—a shoal-ridden stretch of water nearly forty miles long which, because of its numerous wrecks, has long been known as "the graveyard of the Atlantic."

During the late 1920s, when Henry Beston was writing his classic nature book *The Outermost House* on the dunes of Coast Guard Beach, Charlie served as first officer at the Eastham station nearby. He says he knew Beston well ("a real nice feller, very spiffy dresser") and that he is shown in one of the pictures in the first edition. I looked once in my copy, and it contains a photo of an unidentified young officer in dress uniform standing in front of the old station house, but Charlie's name is not on the list of the Eastham crew that Beston gives in the text.

During most of his Coast Guard career, however, he was assigned to the Old Harbor station on North Beach in Chatham. Built about a century ago, this building stood at what was then the entrance to Chatham Harbor, though over the years the entrance has migrated several miles to the south. On that February morning, as I sat with him in his boarded-up shack, Charlie recalled another winter day during his service at Old

Harbor station ("a bit breezier than this one"), when distress flares had been spotted coming from a bark off on the horizon. He and his crew rowed out in the lifeboat to reach the stranded vessel, a distance of some twelve miles, he estimated, over bitter, wintry seas. After they had launched the boat, Charlie discovered that he had forgotten to bring his gloves. Since they couldn't return at that point, he rowed the distance barehanded.

"Fingers almost froze, but I kept workin' them hard all the way out. The swells'd keep throwin' ice up onto the backs of my hands. When we reached her, the captain looks down at my fingers and says, 'You must be cold.' 'Yes, sir, I am,' I says. They made us coffee in the galley—it was all they had. It must have been reheated fifty times, and I don't like coffee anyway, but it tasted good—yes, yes. That bark had been rounding Race Point the night before, but northwest winds tore her sails to pieces and pushed her back down off Chat-ham. We couldn't take anybody off in our boat, and they seemed all right for a bit, so we rowed back, against the wind this time, and called Boston. They sent out the cutter for them. That was the closest one they had in those days."

It was dead cold sitting in that dark shack, for the stove gave out no perceptible heat. I sat huddled in my heavy parka, my gloved hands thrust into my pockets, exhaling thick clouds of vapor into the air. Charlie was dressed in a flannel shirt, down vest, cotton trousers, and boots. He sat relaxed on the plank bench across from me, barehanded and bareheaded, and his breath was invisible.

On another occasion I asked him about an old brick cistern I had found one day half hidden in the thick poplar grove just north of his shack. "Well now," he said, "that was part of Uncle Phil's house used to stand right there in the silverleaf grove. You can still make out the foundation stones around it. Uncle Phil used to own most of the land on this end of Red Top

Road. He had a big barn, too, down the hill where they set off the nitro. We used to have dances in the barn most Saturday nights. Uncle Phil'd hoist a barrel up the old packet pole on top of Signal Hill out back—you don't know about that? Well now, in the old days, before the train come, or even the stage, the only thing comin' to the Cape regular was the packet boat out of Boston. It come more or less regular, depending on the tides and wind, and brought the mail. Well now, most every town on the Bay had a 'signal hill' and a tall pole where they'd run up a flag or a barrel or something so the folks cross-Cape could see when the packet was in. Course there wasn't so many trees then.

"So Uncle Phil'd hoist a barrel up that old pole on Saturday, and folks in the neighborhood'd see it and say, 'Dancin' up to Uncle Phil's tonight.' That house burned down one winter night when both of them were quite old. The barn burned, too, and the horse went up with it. We had quite some times in that old barn—yes, yes."

5

Talking with Lillian Scott the other day, I found myself expressing some rather conventional misgivings about the number of houses, my own included, that had sprung up around Punkhorn in recent years.

"Well now," she answered, in the native's deliberate manner of considering new ways or ideas and trying to fit them into some larger perspective, "there used to be a lot more houses around here than there are now."

I had heard of the Cash house, and of Philip Ellis's place, and of one or two other former dwellings in the neighborhood, but these, it seems, were just the tip of a vanished iceberg. In Brewster's heyday, when a hundred sea captains made their homes along the town's main street, even backwaters like Punkhorn were apparently a good deal more populous than they have been at any other time since until the recent building boom:

"My father, Frank Ellis," said Lillian, "was born in a house way in on a road that's lost now in the woods south of where the Cashes lived. Now Charlie Ellis's place, that's modern. His uncle Phil had a large house right there in the silverleaf grove north of it, but it burned. And down where the Ramseys live on Stony Brook, there used to be a nice little Episcopal chapel in there. The Cashes, before they moved up on the hill behind Jennie Baker's, lived under where the power lines run now. One night the old woman there knocked over a lantern and it burned down. There weren't too many of them left after that, but the town took up a collection and they took to living in Thad Ellis's old house on the hill. That got blown down a few years back. He was the first Ellis around here. You know the Bouchards' house, over to the Dillingham Cemetery. Well now, that's an old cranberry barn belonged to the Ryders. Sam Ryder was in the Civil War, and the house got moved to Chat-ham after the war. The foundation's still there, if you look. Square, too, not round like most of the old ones were. The old school-house that used to be in the meadow down by the herrin' run, that was bought up and moved to Elbow Pond by Lewis Crowell for his cranberryin' business. Nate Black used to work for him there years back. It finally blew down in the '38 hurricane. And of course there was the old Methodist meeting-house in the cemetery. It didn't look much like a church, no steeple or anything, just a regular two-story house. They moved it to East Dennis back before the Civil War because most of the congregation was there by then. It's still there, on Pleasant Street, owned now by a minister named Nyberg, I think. Still has its red roof, too."

We tend to think of old abandoned country houses as gradually decaying, falling apart, their foundations slowly crumbling and filling up the cellar holes, in Frost's phrase, "like a dent in dough." In fact, few country houses today die a natural death. They are more likely to be obliterated in an instant by our machines to make way for new housing tracts and highways. But listening to Lillian, I had the impression that most of the vanished Punkhorn houses had suffered neither fate; they had been burned, blown down, or moved—quick, violent ends or new beginnings elsewhere. Her own house, she told me, had been moved to its present location from East Dennis a hundred years ago.

On Cape Cod, particularly, there is a strong tradition, with practical roots, of moving houses and other buildings. It began in the early nineteenth century because of the scarcity of timber here and the high price of importing lumber. Before the 1850s, when the railroad first arrived down-Cape, it was simply cheaper to move old houses than to build new ones. Long before modular homes manufactured in New Hampshire began traveling down the Mid-Cape Highway in plastic-wrapped halves on flatbed trailers destined for "Captain's Villages," local sea captains were splitting their full Capes in two in order to bequeath them to their children as half-Capes. Half-houses were shoved together to make full Capes with double doors. Buildings were jacked up and carted off on roller logs pulled by teams of oxen, or floated on barges down creeks or even across the Bay.

There is a story about a tavern that used to sit down at Rock Harbor in Orleans in the 1880s, which the owner wanted to move to a new location on the Eastham shore one town up the Bay. That winter, they say, Cape Cod Bay froze over so hard that it was decided to move the tavern across the ice. About halfway across, however, the snow became so heavy that they couldn't make any headway, so they just left it there and did business as usual on the ice for six weeks before finishing the journey.

In Brewster most of the moves were less spectacular, but still quite common. On Main Street there is a small Federal-style house whose front has a curious informal look. The present owner informed me that at one point it had been rolled across the street and left with its backside facing front, since it had been too much trouble to turn around. Other houses were simply shifted, or "squared" to the road, at the request of certain captains' wives, as one might straighten a couch against a wall. Barns, being larger, were not often moved whole, but were commonly disassembled, peg by peg, marked, and reassembled on a new site, the original stones often serving as the new foundation. Smaller sheds and outbuildings went whizzing along the dirt roads, serving time as a slaughterhouse in one town, a stable in another, a fishing shack in yet another.

The tradition is not wholly gone, and even today one occasionally sees an old Cape or summer cottage crawling down the highway on a flatbed trailer, usually in order to make way for some new shopping center or condominium entrance, though the rising costs of moving houses and the proliferating webs of utility wires have made this feat less and less feasible. A few winters ago the Old Harbor Coast Guard Station in Chatham, where Charlie Ellis once served, was sawed in two and floated some twenty miles north on barges to a more stable location in Provincetown, where it now serves as a National Seashore museum.

Perhaps it was just the lack of lumber here, but it may also have been the influence of these ever-shifting shores that led Cape Codders to think of their houses less as family *seats*, founded for the ages, than as temporary shelters, like the borrowed shells of hermit crabs, to be shifted about and exchanged, in location and function, as the need arose. Thoreau's famous image in *Walden* of "a poor immortal soul . . . creeping down the road of life, pushing before it a barn seventy-five feet by forty," was often realized literally here, not only to the material benefit of the owner but perhaps also to his spiritual well-being. It was a community as well as a landscape in motion here, both worn lightly by the inhabitants.

6
_____

Today I live in a place that is being occupied in a sense undreamt of by those who lie in Red Top Cemetery and inconceivable to their remaining descendants. It is a land that we are coming to dominate to such an extent that we no longer recognize what it is we possess or dispossess. Each year the phone books grow thicker, the weekly lists of building permits grow longer, and the face of the landscape, the creation of generations of close, intimate contact between man and nature, grows more indistinct.

No longer do we inherit our homesites or acquire them through marriage. No longer do we hunker down to dig up a handful of soil, squeezing it, smelling it, letting it run through our fingers to find out its texture. An expanding town water system makes it less necessary to determine how far beneath our land the water table lies or what its quality is. In most cases the only contact we have with the deeper nature of the place where we live is a five-minute soil-percolation test, performed by the health agent, to see whether the ground will absorb our wastes at an acceptable rate.

No longer do we estimate the standing cordage of the surrounding trees or ask the location of the nearest spring. Rarely do we inquire into the species of native trees, shrubs, wildflowers, or grasses already on our lot. In recent years landscaping has become a big business on the Cape. Developers spend large amounts of money to import stacks of sod squares from Georgia, piecing them together like green tiles to form an instant lawn on the scraped sandy soil. If their project is big enough, they may even truck in twenty-foot sugar maples or Colorado blue spruces to replace the scraggly, undistinguished pitch pines.

Like Ikey Dunham, I sometimes find myself walking home through the woods, whistling or singing to "keep things away"—though it is not the unseen powers of the night but the all-too-visible forces of the day that scare me.

Yet the longer I live here, the more these burgeoning, current lives of ours seem superficial in the literal sense, merely the most recent face, a veneer, a floating algal scum on the accumulated sea of history of this place. Everywhere around me I see signs of past human use—in the woods, in the bogs, along the roads, on the beaches, and on the flats. Together they make an enduring pattern and a natural, seemly rhythm of alteration, use, withdrawal, and reclamation.

I came to this place originally for reasons that were not false but of necessity partial. It is only by living in a place for a time that we begin to learn where we are. I carved myself a niche in these time-beaten woods with the rev and whine of a chainsaw, the growl and shove of a bulldozer that inevitably precede our arrival on these shores today. Now, after several years, their noise has receded and the scars have begun to heal, and I begin to read some of the old signposts.

Several old abandoned homesteads and foundations still lie hidden in these woods, guarded by lilacs or perhaps by a gnarled and bent mulberry tree brought back from the Pacific in the days of the China trade. Red Top Road still winds its riparian, unpaved course through the low hills, and each year the belichened stone walls plow through a new crop of fallen leaves. A weathered, whitewashed pole still stands on the summit of Signal Hill, though it has been the better part of a century since a barrel was run up its crooked length to announce packets or dances, and the young oaks, having reclaimed the crest, all but swallow up the pole in their rising branches. Nate Black the barber and his wife Emily sleep next door in the little graveyard, where in winter I sometimes find a single line of linked fox tracks winding between the cedars and the headstones. Two generations of his ancestors' bones lie with him, and another two generations of his descendants have already claimed their places nearby with half-dated monuments.

A little farther down Stony Brook Road, a spider spins its web inside a rusty, disused mailbox. The metal flag hangs down, and the faded, painted letters—CONRAD AIKEN— are barely visible. Across the street from 41 Doors, two new houses now sit on the slopes of the poet's "lost Sheepfold Hill," but his "plum tree's seven-branched lyre" still blooms each spring beside the front door and weathered shingles of the ancient farmhouse. Around the back of the house, visible in the window of the upstairs dormer, is an unpainted plaster bust of Aiken. With white, dreaming eyes it looks out over the greening bog below. And each April, when the pink-winks begin to sing in the pools, Charlie Ellis comes by in his blue pickup and rakes away last year's leaves.

So in my mind the various overlapping layers of history, past and recently past, natural and human, blend and fuse together into one rich textured presence, as the accumulated leaffalls finally decay and merge to form new humus. My own life here is only another—the topmost—layer of this human compost, but I will not withhold myself from it for that, though the risks of loving something that has become so vulnerable are great. The call here is great, too, and promises so much. When I look out, I want to see something other than my own face staring back at me.

It is late on a late winter's afternoon, a few weeks after Charlie Ellis explained about the nitroglycerin. I stand at the kitchen sink washing the supper dishes. Out of the window I can see across the road to the poplar grove containing the hidden cistern. The leafless trees are tinged with a rose fire from the setting sun. I stand there for a long while, thinking of the house and the barn that once stood there, and of all the vanished houses and people of Punkhorn. The last of the cold fire climbs the thin, silvered trunks, infusing and consuming the upper branches, and finally leaps from the topmost twigs, disappearing into a winter sky drained of color. Then, over the nippled dome of Signal Hill beyond the trees, there slowly appears a huge full moon that grows and grows like a giant milky bubble until at last it clears the hill and floats, majestically and silently, off to the southeast. And I think to myself, *Dancin' up to Uncle Phil's tonight.*

PART 2

Going Out

CHAPTER 7

Berry's Hole

and before sun-up, and late at night,
the pinkwinks shrill, the pinkwinks trill,
crying from the bog's edge to lost Sheepfold Hill.

—CONRAD AIKEN, "Mayflower"

1

Something has gone wrong with the eggs. The last of the tadpoles is dead. I don't know what happened.

But then, this whole enterprise has been an exercise in ignorance, a kind of catch-up experiment in which I have continuously been at least a day behind the teacher in my preparation. When I first thought of collecting some of the amphibian eggs that appear each spring in the small bog behind my house, I knew little about what I was doing and next to nothing about the different types of eggs I found there or what they might develop into. Whatever I learned, I learned afterward. Collect now, identify later, is the motto of the novice. In a way, I suppose, it made it more exciting, not knowing exactly what I would get.

All I knew was that in late March the shallow, tea-colored waters of the bog in Berry's Hole had become full of small, round, gelatinous clumps of eggs stuck to submerged or floating objects. On the first of April, I put on long rubber boots and waded carefully out into the water. Slogging around in the soft bottom muck, I used a small minnow net to pluck the globular egg masses, like overripe fruit, from the twigs and stones to which they were attached, and lowered them carefully into a pail.

When I had gathered a pailful, I picked through my collection, keeping three of the most visibly different masses and placing the rest back into the water. The enveloping jelly of the smallest mass, about the size of a tennis ball, had a white fuzzy cast, as though it were covered with a mold. The larger two, the size of Osage oranges, were clear and contained about a hundred eggs each. Carrying them back up the slope and into the house, I put each egg mass into its own jar of bog water, placed the three jars inside a small aquarium half full of tap water, and set the whole assembly on top of the piano in the living room.

There they floated, eggs inside jars inside the glass aquarium. I sat on the piano bench and looked at them through six separate shells of air, glass, water, and transparent outer jelly. Yet I could clearly see not only each perfectly round individual egg but also within each egg a dark, distinct yolk, nut brown with a slight golden cast, already partly split in two, like a pair of tiny clamshells. At once deeply enfolded and naked to sight, how different these amphibian eggs are from our own dark and invisible gestations!

The egg masses themselves had the look of miniature clouds with soiled tops, seeded with the germs of frogs or salamanders—I had no idea which at the time. But they floated there, heavy with promise, feeling, as the days went by, Mozart or Gershwin or Billy Joel hammered out beneath them, dreaming and formless, waiting to uncurl, blossom, twitch, and fall to life.

2
_____

Berry's Hole is the most prominent topographical feature in the immediate neighborhood. It is a large, circular depression, roughly a thousand feet across and ninety feet from the top of the surrounding ridges to the bog at its bottom. Like hundreds of other kettle holes of varying sizes that pockmark the morainal ridges and outwash plains of Cape Cod, Berry's Hole is essentially a fossil iceberg.

When the last ice sheet to cover this corner of North America retreated, some 12,000 years ago, large chunks of the main mass broke off and were subsequently covered over with glacial till and debris spread by the meltwater runoff. Thus insulated, these huge ice blocks remained frozen for some time after the glacier had departed and left the Cape a bleak and barren pile of rubble. When at last these buried icebergs melted, the ground above them sank to form the bowllike depressions of various sizes known as kettle holes. When the bottoms of these holes lie above the surrounding groundwater table, they are dry hollows; when they lie below it, they are ponds.

The bog at the bottom of Berry's Hole is on the borderline between a temporary pool and a permanent wetland. Although it usually contains some water, the amount fluctuates both seasonally and annually. If we have had a rainy fall and all the leaves are down, and if I stand on top of the stone wall that runs along our back property line, stretch up on my toes, and peer down the slope that drops off below, I just might manage to catch, through the maze of twigs and branches, a fleeting glimpse of open water at the bottom. Conditional as it is, it is probably the closest I will ever come to owning waterview property.

The bog surface is normally about 150 feet on its longest axis, though during dry summers the water level may sink completely out of sight, leaving only a moist floor of caked mud. During the mid-1960s Cape Cod, along with most of New England, experienced one of the worst droughts in its history. Longtime residents in the area have told me that Berry's Hole remained virtually dry then for several years in succession, which eliminated most of its aquatic life. In years of abundant rainfall, however, the bog may hold several feet of dark, acidic water and produce bumper crops of frogs, salamanders, mosquitoes, and aquatic insects.

In the center of the bog is a small island of established shrubs and small swamp maples, where in summer I regularly find the nests of red-winged blackbirds and song sparrows and occasionally that of a black-and-white warbler. The bog's perimeter is fringed with thick stands of highbush blueberry and black alder, or winterberry, whose brilliant scarlet-orange berries remain on the branches throughout the winter, providing food for chickadees and titmice and a festive necklace for the otherwise dead aspect of the bog. Near the edges there are also some fairly large maples, but farther up the sides of the kettle hole the oaks predominate, except for one stand of beeches on the steeper, southwest slope.

In September and October the bog is often host to migrating waterfowl—black ducks, mallards, an occasional teal—which use its shallow waters as a rest stop, remaining from a few hours to several days or more. Sometimes I can observe them undetected from the wooded edges around the bog, but when I startle them, they leap up quacking, lifting their plump bodies effortlessly and nearly vertically up and over the rim of the bowl like feathered balloons.

In winter, if the water level remains high, the bog provides the neighborhood children with a moderately decent skating pond; and one year I was inspired to clear a toboggan run down from our house. By late January the mating calls of the resident great horned owls begin to rise up out of the hole at night. Male and female together, they utter long, unseen duets, deep antiphonal hootings whose voices move slowly toward one another under the Snow Moon.

Thus Berry's Hole possesses a broad, diastolic rhythm, swelling and contracting its waters and various lives throughout the seasons and from year to year. Compared with the ocean's tides or the rise and fall of great rivers, its fluctuations are modest, at most a few feet between extremes of wetness and drought. Yet for its size the tides of life that it supports are prodigious, rising at times to overflow the confines of its wooded slopes, lapping at the very windows of our houses in seasons of flood, then ebbing, contracting, drawing at last a cover of icy silence over itself in winter.

3

In late February the bog still lies silent and ice covered, yet already I begin to sense a movement, a deep, hidden stirring in the frozen earth. All across the dead landscape, a vast terrestrial vernal migration is about to start. Moved by the gradual thawing of the earth, the warming rains, and the dictates of their own biological clocks, the Cape's hibernating amphibians will begin crawling out from under leaf litter, from under the bark of dead trees, from deathlike entombments several feet underground. Moving for the most part unseen and unheard, this parade of wood frogs, newts, spotted and woodland salamanders, spring peepers and gray tree frogs, Fowler's and American toads, and, in odd years, enormous numbers of a strange primitive amphibian known as the spadefoot toad will be drawn toward the thousands of small, boggy, weedy pools that lace the Cape's cutover woodlands and bushy undergrowth, reaffirming their ancient aquatic origins by the need to lay their eggs in water.

Much of this migratory activity in our neighborhood is focused on the dark funnel of Berry's Hole, which in spring becomes a glory hole for frogs and salamanders. Its attraction for these creatures is due in large part to its own amphibious nature. Too shallow to support a permanent fish population— the prime predators of amphibian eggs—it is much more reliable as a wetland than are most temporary spring pools. As the melting snows and cold rains of early spring raise its waters, it becomes a body of great magnetism, drawing to itself the returning land migrants in a gradually growing mass of sound and excitement until at last it seems to explode and fling its concentrated life back out again.

In early March, not long after the rusty-voiced redwings start showing off their flashy epaulets in the marshes and the beaked spadices of the skunk cabbage have burned their way up through the icy mud of stream and swamp borders, strange, wooden, quacking noises begin to rise out of the bog. These odd-sounding calls belong to one of the most handsome and charming of all woodland amphibians, the wood frog. It is the woodfrog, and not the more-celebrated spring peeper, that is the first New England frog to break the ice of winter's silence. In some years I have even found its splay-toed prints in late snow around the bog's border.

About two inches long, the adult frog occurs in color phases that roughly span the spectrum of cedar shingles as they weather: from light sandy red to pale silver gray. It has a distinct white upper lip and a characteristic black mask that extends on each side of the head from the snout through the lower half of the eye and over the tympanum, the frog's external eardrum.

Of all our local frogs, the wood frog depends most on wetlands such as Berry's Hole, for it will establish permanent populations only around temporary or semipermanent ponds. In areas where such seasonal wetlands have been filled in, dredged out, or converted to cranberry bogs, the numbers of wood frogs have declined drastically or disappeared altogether.

One day in mid-March, while Beth and I were having lunch indoors, we heard wood frogs quacking away down in the hole like a flock of mallards. It was an unusually warm and sunny day, so we left our food, went outside, and walked down to see them. As we neared the bog, the frogs suddenly ceased calling, as we knew they would, but we could see their light, tan-colored bodies floating on the tea-colored water. They lay passively at the surface, with the reflections of white clouds all around them, drifting across the bog, like brown autumn leaves against the blue sky. As I stepped to the edge of the water, several of the frogs dove and kicked their way with strong, repeated strokes to the bottom, where they hid beneath sunken leaves. Water boatmen, also the first of the season, sculled their smooth, hull-like bodies backward across the dark water.

A light wind was blowing, cutting all things loose from their winter moorings. It scattered broken chords of sunlight across the water and blew gently against our cheeks. The kettle hole gathered warmth down into itself from a rising sun that beat its way across the great cerulean mixing bowl of the sky. Earth and sky, old coolness and new warmth, the rocking quarters of the year, all seemed to play seesaw with one another, and even love seemed to go more lightly. We stood for a long time at the bottom of the kettle hole watching the wood frogs drift like leaves across the bog, and then climbed slowly back up to the house.

That day marked the beginning of a warming trend that lasted for a full week, a great river of southwest wind hundreds of miles long that washed over the land, mopping up the remaining spots and patches of the last snowfall, breaking winter's back for good, and taking full possession of the land, though the visible signs of spring remained elusive.

Then one night there came a madness from the hole as the peepers joined the wood frogs in full breeding chorus for the first time. Wood frogs generally utter their rapid *brek-kek-kek-kek* calls most loudly and frequently on sunny days, while the peepers tend to reach their tutti fortissimos on warm, rainy nights. Frequently, however, they overlap, with the peepers providing a subdued daytime chorus to the much fewer wood frogs, and the wood frogs in turn punctuating the peepers' deafening nocturnal chants.

After dinner I walked outside and stood at the brink of the slope, breasting the flow of soft air that carried their song. It was a wild, primitive sound, a mixture of bells and castanets, with an underlying urgent rhythm such as great flocks of nesting or roosting birds possess. Listening to their collective voice rising out of that dark throat into the night, I felt once again that spring is the season of ignorance.

If we are aware at all of the myriad new sounds that sift out of the air and seep up from the ground at this time of year, we are generally satisfied with naming them, or at most with learning some basic facts about their origin or means of production. I know, for instance, that the spring peeper is a small, inch-long tree frog with a crosslike marking on its back that gives it its species name, *Hyla crucifer*. It is widespread and abundant over the entire Cape, and each March the male peepers gather in large numbers in virtually every pond, bog, and seasonal wetland, uttering their high, thin pipings together at night to attract mates.

In chorus, the peeper's song carries a remarkable distance. I once lived in a comparatively dry area of town, with no nearby pools, even in wet seasons. Yet one evening I heard the distant, bell-like chanting of these frogs from my front step and decided to track it down. I finally arrived at a small drainage pool in back of a filling station nearly half a mile away.

What enables such a tiny animal to produce such a prodigious noise is its distensible throat, or vocal sac. The frog inhales air into this sac, which swells up into an almost transparent bubble nearly as large as itself. Then, keeping its mouth closed, it shunts the air back and forth across its vocal chords between throat and lungs, using the sac as a resonating chamber to produce about one peep per second.

If I go only this far, however, I can listen to their yearly singing with a complacence that is probably worse than no knowledge at all. Each spring, for several years, I used to produce a series of local radio programs on bird songs, and yet I realize I am at a loss to explain the simplest facts about this primitive amphibian and its song. It is a song older and more impersonal than the robin's cheerful greeting, or that of any bird. It is older, for that matter, than the crocus, the violet, or any flower. It is older, by hundreds of millions of years, than Cape Cod itself. It may, according to some evolutionists, be the oldest sound of spring in existence, and yet we know next to nothing about it.

Why do frogs sing? Apparently their song does serve to attract females to the breeding site, though the evidence for this is unclear. Unlike birds, frogs have great difficulty in distinguishing one pitch from another. In the wild they frequently try to mate with members of other species, and they also respond to sounds well outside the amphibian range—such as the noises of passing planes and fire engines, or bad human imitations. Species like the wood frog and the spring peeper, which share breeding grounds, may have evolved their relatively separate singing times in order not to further confuse the tone-deaf females.

Some scientists have suggested that frog singing expresses a primitive sort of territoriality. Indeed, on the few occasions when I have managed to observe peepers singing at night, the tiny vocalists were usually spaced several feet apart from one another. Buy why should frogs, who do not care for their young, need territories? Charles M. Bogart, a biologist specializing in amphibian song, makes the interesting suggestion that such territorial spacing may help a male frog to recognize a female in his territory. Apparently, batrachian love is literally blind; males frequently mistake other males for prospective mates. To deal with this, many species, especially toads, have developed two distinctive mating calls: one given by a receptive female just before copulation and another, a warning call, uttered by a male that has been mistakenly clasped by an ardent but myopic suitor—a kind of "Right! Right!" and "Wrong! Wrong!" signal system.

But even in the light of these tentative explanations, singing in frogs appears to be an unnecessary extravagance. After all, other amphibians, notably the salamanders and the eellike caecilians, are virtually voiceless and yet manage perfectly well to get together in their watery breeding places without noisy fanfare. Could it be that, as has been suggested regarding birds, the frogs to some extent simply "enjoy" their gravelly harmony?

For that matter, though, should we even call such noises "song"? Of the frogs and toad calls I have listened to, those with a more or less definite pitch, like the peeper's, lack any recognizable individual rhythm, while those with fairly definite rhythms, like the wood frog's, are toneless and dry. Most lack both tone and rhythm. Yet whatever aesthetic reservations we may have about them, frogs do tend to sing in large numbers, and the effect of the whole is often more than the sum of its croaks. En masse and from a distance, for example, the sound of peepers carries a definite, if elusive, shape and rhythm that Robert Frost called "a ghost of sleighbells in a ghost of snow." At closer range, however, the impression can be quite different.

As I descended from the top of the slope down into the dark hollow thick with singing peepers, it was as though I were entering some vast three-dimensional pointillistic painting. As I approached the bottom of the hole, the aggregate forms of sound broke up and resolved themselves into individual dots of song. Finally, down at the bog's edge, I was surrounded by what seemed like a million separate pipings, higher, clearer, and more piercing than they were from above. Nor was their sound as simple as I had thought. I began to notice a soft murmuring, inaudible at any distance, that preceded the peep— something like the soft wooden *thock* that introduces the whippoorwill's strident call. Occasionally the peep note itself was varied by a quick, rising trill: *pr-e-e-e-eeep*!

Sometimes, when I have brought along a flashlight, I have been lucky enough to spot a peeper singing, more often from a low-hanging branch than in the water itself, its white, swollen, translucent throat pumping away beneath imperturbable jeweled eyes. Now, however, as is usually the case, I could see nothing. The tiny frogs remained maddeningly invisible, while their song was everywhere. So possessed were they that even my near approach failed to quiet them, but only created a momentary bubble of silence around me that was already closing back in. The sound seemed to flow around me as I stood at the edge of the bog. I knew they were within a few feet of me, perhaps right at my feet. But the frogs' natural camouflage and the ventriloquial quality of their song made the sound as indeterminate as it was manifest.

After several minutes the peeping seemed to be emanating from directly inside my head, the way monophonic music does when listened to through a set of stereo earphones. The swelling noise expanded and occupied the seat of thought itself, growing in intensity until it was like a million neurons popping and discharging inside my brain.

So *this*, I thought, is what a frog hears, night after night, week after week! This maddening, dionysian ubiquity of sound, which we for the most part experience as a gentle, lilting background to the season, and in the deafness of our distance call cold-blooded!

4
___

Whatever its ultimate purpose or true nature, the apparent result of all this sound and fury is those protruding jelly balls of eggs that first appeared with the wood frogs in mid-March and grew in number until the entire bog began to look like a thick dumpling stew. I later learned, however, that none of the egg masses I had collected at the beginning of April were peeper eggs. A fierce individualist in this respect, each female peeper lays her thousand or so eggs one at a time, attaching them singly to the underside of rocks and sunken branches. If possible, peeper eggs are even harder to find than the adults that lay them.

Ironically, the greatest volume of egg matter in Berry's Hole is produced by the amphibian that makes the least noise about it—in fact, no noise at all. The spotted salamander has a glistening, jet-black body seven or eight inches long with bright, distinct orange-yellow spots. It looks and feels like a glazed rubber dime-store animal, painted by someone whose lunch break was coming up and who had little concern for the fineness of detail and subtle shading that we associate with most living creatures. They come to the little bog by the hundreds in spring. I frequently find their squashed, still-wriggling forms along the nearby highways or see them moving like stubby blacksnakes through new lawns. One evening in mid-April, in a pattering rain, I walked down into the bog and entered again the almost-palpable chanting of the peepers. As usual I saw no frogs, but at the edge of the water, wriggling in and out of the submerged leaves, were half a dozen salamanders. They were males, I guessed, actively laying down spermatophores, which the females would subsequently absorb into their cloacae to fertilize their eggs. Then, in a convincing display of salamandrine curiosity, they all stopped what they were doing and lined up at the shore edge, staring up at my flashlight from under the water with unblinking, bulging eyes.

April continued unusually wet. Night after night it rained hard, heavy downpours that were wonderful to listen to, that raised the water level in the bog and the peeper chorus to new heights with spits and spatters, lashings and drummings, tappings and surges. The hole filled and erupted with soughs, bendings, and little skyrockets of sound—wind, rain, and frog song—all the orchestrated passion of inanimate energy and ancient life.

Indoors, inside the jars in the aquarium on the piano, the first of the eggs had hatched from one of the two larger masses about a week after I had collected them. They were salamander larvae: small, speckled teardrops with red external gills stuck to the sides of their necks like tiny, red gloves. By the end of the second week, several more salamanders had hatched from the second large mass. Most of the embryos, however, sank down in their transparent shells, their limp, gray bodies conforming to the rounded bottoms. There in their egg coffins they slowly deteriorated, unhatched. But this, I felt, was to be expected; most animals that lay large numbers of eggs experience high mortality before birth.

After another week some eggs from the third, smaller mass had hatched. I removed the jars, sectioned the aquarium into three compartments with nylon screen, and filled it with water brought up from the bog, making sure that it contained plenty of bottom detritus, surface algae, and microorganisms for food. Then, carefully, I siphoned up the hatched larvae from each jar with a turkey baster and placed them into separate compartments.

In the meantime other life began to emerge from the woods and bogs, creeping over the road edges and out onto the pavement. Blacksnakes slithered along the streets. Armored snapping turtles crawled out of the swamps and moved ponderously, like miniature dinosaurs, across highways to lay their eggs in some sandy bank. Skunks and opossums hunched their way out of the darkness and along roadsides on their way toward some gruesome midnight feast. At night, in the glare of my headlights, herds of blanched tree frogs performed grotesque skeletal jigs on the rain-pelted asphalt. All over the town, at every low dip or bend in the roads, the peeper chants penetrated rolled-up car windows and sealed wills, reminding us that we are not alone.

By the first week in May the salamander larvae were about an inch long and had developed small, three-toed forelegs just below the feathered gills, as well as embryonic hindleg bumps halfway down their tail sections. Of the twenty or so young hatched from the two larger egg masses, all had so far survived. In addition, there were now three good-sized larvae from the third mass, which I had identified as wood-frog tadpoles. Almost black in color and typically polliwog-shaped, they were about twice the size of the salamanders. The tadpoles appeared to be developing their hindlegs first, and much farther down on their bodies. Every few days I refilled the aquarium with fresh bog water and awaited the next transformation.

On the ninth of May a new season—call it True Spring, Leaf Time, or Warbler Weather—was ushered in on waves of soft, bugless air from the south. For the first time the temperature rose into the seventies and stayed there. At night the moon stood high and nearly full. Leaves bubbled at the brink, ready to gush out. Every oak crown had become a feathery plume, dusting the soft stars overhead. The peeper chorus, though beginning to subside, still rose strongly out of the bog below, while whippoorwills cracked their sharp calls from the dark hillsides. The far sloping rim of the kettle hole still stood out sharply against a planetarium sky, though within a week it would once more be blotted out by leaves. From beyond the rim, in a hidden meadow nearly half a mile away, came the spaced, buzzlike calls of a moonstruck woodcock as the bird rose in starry spirals of its courtship flight. Over the burgeoning treetops the toads began dry, toneless screaming. It was all a wonderful seasonal fugue, a passing on of verbal torches through the spring months, old ones going out, new ones being lit, under the night's perfection.

5
——————

But something has gone wrong with the eggs. One of the salamanders was born noticeably malformed, its body bent into a permanent curve, so that it was able only to thrash about in circles. Its growth, too, appeared stunted. While the tails of its siblings grew longer and more pointed, its own remained a rounded stump. Yet surprisingly, it managed to survive, drawing sustenance from the bog-water debris even in its crippled state.

Another salamander larva had a ballast problem. It could not seem to stay on the bottom of the aquarium and was constantly floating up to the surface. Each time it struggled back down, only to bob up again. Yet it, too, somehow survived.

Then, shortly after that warm night in early May, everything inside the aquarium came to a mysterious halt. Outside, during the weeks that followed, the wood-frog chorus died out completely, orioles and wood thrushes returned, mayflowers bloomed and turned brown on the hillsides, paper wasps began building their honeycomb nests under the eaves—but the salamander larvae simply swam around or hid in the bottom debris of the aquarium. The tumult of the peepers gradually diminished to an occasional peep, woodcocks continued to dance under a full moon, the screaming of the gulls announced the running of the herring in Stony Brook, but the wood-frog tadpoles only wriggled about in endless circles with round, grape-size heads, small undeveloped hindlegs that appeared tucked up under their ears, and black stringlike tails.

Salamander larvae and terrestrial-frog tadpoles are designed to metamorphose completely in a matter of weeks, even several days if necessary, in temporary wetlands. The remaining egg masses in Berry's Hole had disappeared weeks ago, and presumably its leaf-littered slopes were now hopping and

crawling with tiny new peepers, wood frogs, and salamanders
on their way to whatever summer rendezvous they were pro-
grammed for. Yet my amphibians seemed to have entered a
state of arrested development.

What had gone wrong? What had caused this shutdown?
Was the food supply in the bog water insufficient? Was some
essential vitamin or mineral missing? Was the water too cold?
Too warm? Was there not enough oxygen?

One obvious suspect was "acid rain," that spreading national
malady of sulfurous and nitrous air pollutants which has
increased the acidity of several of our Cape ponds to a level
that is lethal to many aquatic organisms, including amphibians. According to one herpetologist whom I consulted, spotted salamanders are particularly sensitive to increased acidity,
which can inhibit calcium formation in the larvae.

Bogs are, of course, naturally acidic, but a litmus-paper test
of the water showed a pH of roughly 4.0, which is classified as
"critically acid" for pond water. The test, however, was done
shortly after a week of heavy rainfall, and so might reflect a
higher acidity than that of the underlying water table.

There were also, I realized, any number of other conditions,
in the bog or in the aquarium, that might have been responsible for the larvae's arrested development. I even wondered
whether it might have been a bad idea to have placed them on
the piano, whether the eggs had somehow been damaged by
their musical substrate of juvenile exercises and bad adult playing.

But the truth is that, in the end, I simply was not suffi-
ciently interested to pursue the matter further. All I knew was
that the larvae had ceased to change. After a while I gradually
lost interest and often went for a week or more without even
looking at them. But as June rolled on I started to question my
right to keep them any longer. They had now been living on top
of my piano for two and a half months. My manner of keep-

ing them obviously had no scientific value. It had been purely for my personal curiosity, and even that had been waning fast.

Unaccountably, I found myself beginning to get irritated at the little creatures. It may have had something to do with the fact that with each passing week the clouds of emerging mosquitos at the bottom of Berry's Hole grew thicker, making the task of getting fresh bog water increasingly unpleasant. Or maybe it was just that it was time to be getting on to a new season, and these wood-frog tadpoles and salamander larvae represented a stalemate, a stagnation of the year, that was keeping me from moving into summer.

Then, on top of everything else, they began to suffer attrition. During the last two weeks of June, the twenty surviving salamander larvae were reduced to eight, and two out of the three frog tadpoles died. I could never find any of the bodies; they just seemed to disappear.

Just as I was about to give up on them and return the remaining young to the bog, the last tadpole metamorphosed overnight. I found it in the morning, a small frog less than an inch long, with faint parallel streaks on its legs, lateral ridges along its warty back, and a general sandy color, though it still lacked the adult's face markings. With a small net I lifted it out of the aquarium and placed it in a shallow white enameled pan of water. In the middle of the pan I set a small rock. The frog climbed up onto the rock and never again got back in the water.

That afternoon I took an inch-long cabbageworm from the garden and placed it on the rock beside the frog. The worm reared up and touched the frog, which instantly panicked and leaped a good eighteen inches across the top of the piano. I removed the worm and placed the frog back on the rock.

Aside from that one frightened leap, the frog never again moved or seemed to pay any attention to anything around it. It simply remained sitting on the rock in the middle of the pan of water, motionless except for its regularly pumping throat, staring out into space with those bejeweled golden eyes, as though waiting for something beyond this room, beyond this house, some release or fulfillment I could not or would not give it.

It came the next morning, a warm, bright summer's day in late June. I found the frog floating belly up in the pan, limbs limp and extended in the clean water. Its throat was still, and I could see clearly now the black mask of the wood frog beginning to darken into identity across the open, staring eyes.

6

So at last I stepped into summer, and with it came a sustained drought that browned the surrounding hills and nearly sucked the bog dry. During July, Berry's Hole became a green, simmering stew; the broad moat of dark water that had surrounded the center island of shrubs now was an almost unbroken ring of lush grass and rushes two feet high with game trails running through it. The flood of spring had been transformed into this surge of summer foliage—rush, brier, and vine—gushing up in stalks and leaves, flowing invisibly back into the atmosphere.

By August, however, the lushness was gone. Only a single small puddle of open water remained at one end of the bog, and even this pool was covered with a thick scum of algae. Now and then, a few belated wood-frog calls rose from the hole: loose, sporadic clacks that sounded like soggy, leftover firecrackers.

On most days a loud pervasive hum hung over the bog, shutting out any thoughts of visiting it. In summer the hordes of mosquitoes, deerflies, and gnats possess the hole unchallenged. Only when a rare Canadian high brought in a few days of cool, dry weather could I make brief forays down to the bog, hoping to catch a glimpse of one of its seasonal specialties: a green heron stalking through matted waters or a summer tanager glowing in deep, mapled shade. But soon I would be shut out again by a new blanket of buzzing humidity.

Sultry but rainless days followed one another in a long string that seemed to stretch out interminably. In the afternoons a small breeze would struggle partway down the slope, stirring the oak branches briefly; the leaves would lift halfheartedly in response, then hang limp again. Dog days. Yet even the neighborhood dogs were quieted. At long intervals one might be heard beyond the rim, crying mournfully in the distance. It would keep it up for a minute or two, but getting no response, would give up the effort.

The birds were all silent, undergoing a decrease in hormonal production and a vulnerable period of molt prior to migration. All things, in fact, seemed to have settled down to a period of uneventful growth, dull maturation, or premature death. My blood grew thick and heavy with the air. My limbs drooped and pulled me down, like the apple boughs ripening on the crest of the kettle hole. My eyes began to glaze over with a dull film, like the surface of the bog below, and even my mind felt itself being slowly eaten away, like the leaves, with rot and insects.

With September, however, the rains returned, and with them the first waves of fall migrants. One day I found the bog full of grackles, energetically bathing in its waters, dipping and fluttering as the afternoon sun fell from their wet, sheeny shoulders. As I approached them, they took off up the slope in great whooshing volleys, successive blasts of winged grapeshot, a hundred or more birds in each burst, black blurs across my field of vision.

Late in the month a pair of wood ducks—rare migrants on the Cape—settled into the bog for nearly a week. They are surpassingly beautiful birds, though they actually possess much less color than many other ducks that do not begin to approach them in splendor. Their bright plumage is limited, in the male, to an iridescent green head, light blue primaries, red-orange bill, and ruby eye. But the body is marked with thick streaks of stage white, dramatically accenting and contrasting the plumage and giving the bird a strange, ritualistic appearance, like that of a gilded artifact. I always expect them to spout poetry, or at least sing lyrically; instead they emit only high, rabbitlike squeaks.

By the first of October the wood ducks had gone, borne south, I supposed, by the cold front that had come in the night before. Now the bog, swollen by autumn rains, once more had the appearance of a small pond. I stood at its edge, listening to the big swamp maples tick off their leaves one by one down through the twigs and branches, like the slow sand falls on the outer beach. The leaves fell half heads, half tails, into the black, calm water, riding there like little open boats with stems stuck up for masts. Soon they would sink and add another year's compost to the thick organic mat of decaying vegetation that lines the bottom of the bog.

There was a light breeze in the air, but the water was calm and the light clear. This sidewise slanting light in late fall reveals many things invisible under the shadowless summer sun. It etches life into stark, yet warm, relief, showing me again the form of things. Over the dark surface of the bog swarmed clouds of tiny, light-colored gnats, reminding me of a sunlit room full of dust motes. The minuscule insects landed frequently on the water surface, appearing to graze on the even more minute particles of detritus-dust that glazed it. So light were they that they made not the slightest dimple on the glassy expanse, while the larger whirligigs and water boatmen skated and sculled across the film of surface tension, broadcasting patterns of movement as they went.

The shrubs in the bog's center, the surrounding blueberry and alder bushes, and the overhanging trees were all strung with the silken gossamer of wind-borne spiderlings. Glistening and undulating in the afternoon breeze, these ephemeral cables formed a kind of sylvan telegraph system, carrying the mute message that, even for such sedentary creatures as spiders, autumn is the season for dispersals and journeys. The air over the Cape was thick with flying spiderlings, migrating swallows, curlews, warblers and monarch butterflies, sea scoters and broad-winged hawks, blown thistle and milkweed seed. All things seemed to say *leave*, and on that day I was in a mood to listen to them.

This kind of late-autumn weather always tempts me in a way spring fever is supposed to, but rarely does. Perhaps it is because in spring I know where everything is headed: here, toward myself. Spring is essentially narcissistic and centripetal: the gathering of pent-up energy, a concentration of identity and intensity within each living creature until the self must spill over, in sex or song, to be caught and held in the deep, concave satiety of summer.

But this flying off or sinking away to places unseen, unknown, is something I long to be part of. I know what lies beyond the spring of my life, but I have not yet followed autumn's centrifugal mystery to its end. To be torn away, leaf by leaf; to rise, carried on the wind, like the newly fledged shorebirds, who set off on migrations thousands of miles long to places of new beginnings, never seen, yet remembered somewhere in the blood; to follow the downward turning of the year to the old death and new birth somewhere beyond the lines of sight—ah, *that* would be something different, and worth the journey.

7

With November the bog looks emptier than ever. The last of the migrants have flown, the insects have disappeared, and the waters have gathered the remaining leaves and the sinking foliage. Berry's Hole is preparing for winter.

Yet one thing, at least, returns to the bog this time of the year. On certain warm days in late October and early November, when the oaks and hickories have all turned honey colored and russet, when the days dawn clouded and obscure but brighten through the morning into moist, hazy sunshine and a pungent smell of leaf decay hangs in the air, the trees in the hole become filled with a high, thin piping. It is a steady, measured, unexuberant song, plaintive and scattered, like ghost echoes of summer's departed birds.

But these are no ghosts and no birds, though in a sense they are an echo of spring. These are the peepers, the *Hylae*, the same tiny frogs whose concentrated and rhythmic spring chorus filled the throat of Berry's Hole last April and May with a deafening alleluia of trills. Silent and invisible in the woods all summer, they characteristically reappear on late-Indian-summer days for an attenuated reunion of sorts.

The sound is familiar, reminiscent of their first, tentative tunings-up in March, but the location now is unexpected and at first surprising. They pipe from the topmost branches of the oaks and maples, as though to remind me that they are true members of the family of tree frogs. They sing best on warm, moist days when there is haze or mist in the air and the thick odor of rotting vegetation makes me feel as though I were underwater, at the bottom of some deep but thin, soupy swamp, listening to the frogs singing at the surface far above me. This tree serenade is often loudest in mid-November, intermingling with the chipmunks' whistle-thocks and the last cricket stridulations, and may persist until the first frost drives the tiny frogs under leaf mold or old boards for the winter.

This is also the time of year, especially on rainy nights, when these latter-day peepers are likely to show up on my glass doors, plastered there by their suction-cupped feet like August moths. In fact, tree frogs are said to be fond of policing house windows at night in search of insects attracted by the indoor lights, though in late fall the insect pickings are pretty slim.

The other night I looked up from the table and found three

of them hanging on the doors, their Buster Keaton faces pressed up against the glass as though observing me. All summer I had sought them fruitlessly in the woods, and now they had come to me on their own to present themselves, under glass, as it were, for my inspection. I got up and went over to look at them: monkeylike creatures with long, outstretched limbs, agilely stalking the smooth, wet outside surface of the glass, surprisingly complete and flexible for things so small. One was attached in the middle of the sliding panel, about three feet from the bottom. Another was stuck to the upper part of the stationary door near the outside thermometer, as though it had come to take a reading. The third frog sat on the sill at the bottom. The two on the glass were the usual, flecked, grayish green color, while the one on the sill was a lighter shade, almost that of sandstone. The crosses on their backs were faintly visible, as were the fold marks on their white, deflated throat sacs.

The frogs seemed abstracted, almost in a trance. When I slid open the moving door and closed it again, the frog on that panel showed no response to its ride. I tapped on the glass directly in front of it, but if I inspired any fear or alarm, it all seemed concentrated in the frog's throat, which palpitated rapidly like a fevered pulse or a motor on fast idle.

Were these frogs taking any cognizance of me, or was it all a one-way inspection? They moved so freely across the verticle black rectangles of glass that, for a moment, I had the odd sense that I was looking up at them from below, that the doors were the surface of some pond at night and I some submarine creature, some dragonfly larva or water beetle they might be contemplating with their impassive, glittering eyes. They hung there patiently, or moved like spiders across the dark eyes of my house, crouching in the crevices of pane and sash.

I wonder a good deal about the reappearance of the peepers in late autumn, for it is a phenomenon that occurs with a regularity that deserves more recognition and more explanation than I have been able to find. I used to think it was just some remembrance of spring that drew them out, as birds sometimes revive their spring songs during cools spells in late summer. So, I reasoned, these warm, misty days and nights might be sending down their primitive spinal cords some shuddering memory of desire, rousing them to this late woodland piping.

But I think now that it must be more than that, more than just involuntary hormonal nostalgia. For one thing, it seems to be something they share with other local residents at this time of the year. Only yesterday I saw half a dozen woolly-bear caterpillars shuffling across the town tennis courts. There have been all sorts of road kills along Stony Brook Road this past week, and several of my neighbors have reported grouse crashing into their windows. Is it simple population pressures that cause these dispersals in our local wildlife in the fall or some type of unrecognized migration I do not comprehend?

What sets all these animals in motion, what send them on their way? It is, as I have said, an urge I share with them this time of year, even if I do not understand it in myself either. Only the other night, driving home from a friend's house after midnight under a clearing sky and a full moon, I saw not only white frogs but white woodchucks, white rabbits, and white squirrels leaping across the barreled glare of my headlights in a complex and ghostly ballet. Had I not been so tired and sleepy, I might have pulled off the road and followed them into the dark woods.

Instead, I fell asleep thinking about the peepers. They seem to be concentrating around the bog now, though unlike strictly aquatic frogs, they do not hibernate underwater. But perhaps they nestle under the leaves in the general proximity of their breeding pools. Do these terrestrial frogs, like salmon and alewives, return to the pool where they were born? Many of these frog ponds have been dry since early summer and reappear only now, in late fall, which might help to account for the sudden general movement toward them. Why the frogs would do this, I have no idea. Maybe they do it so as not to forget their pool's location, or even their own existence, during their long winter sleep.

In their apparent cycles of movement to and from the hole—their intense spring concentrations, sudden dispersals, mysterious summer disappearances, and autumnal regroupings—the peepers seem a type of exploding universe, expanding and contracting, only to explode again each spring. Or is there a different and less complex explanation? Could these fall frogs merely be the year's new generation, late-emerging adults who manage to leave the bogs only with time enough to pipe a few tenatative notes before going to sleep? Who knows Hyla? Who has studied these frog migrations? Has anyone ever taken a Christmas frog count, digging them up in midwinter around a known breeding pond? Why is it that we know so little about our nearest, oldest, and most abiding neighbors?

8

November went out with the first bite of winter in its mouth. Several cold, clear nights at the end of the month put a thin skim of ice on the smaller wetlands on the first of December, and on that morning I went down into the hole again to have a look. The water level in the bog had sunk quite a bit during the preceding week, as though shrunken with the cold, and its shores were rimmed with a wide band of exposed, crinkly gray leaves. The covering of ice was black, cracked in a complex pattern of intersecting geometric shapes—narrow trapezoids, truncated pyramids, long shards of glass with inverted points—all the straight and bent lines of the forming crystals, the "bones of the ice," as Thoreau called them. The impression was of a large black-satin sheet left unsmoothed across the bog, or that of an enormous black-veined dragonfly's wing.

Though paper-thin, the ice represented the first seal on the bog's watery life, a transparent operculum drawn down over its soft, summer foot. It was hard to realize that only a week earlier I had listened to the high pipings of peepers in the trees around its perimeter. Where was Hyla now? Asleep, folded into the leaf-littered slopes, secure in its seasonal oblivion, dreaming the rounded, diastolic contours of its life.

But I was left above ground, to witness what I could. Over the dam of the southeastern slope the rush of winter sunlight began to fill the hole with a loud roaring. I could hear the sharp *zeet-zeet-zeet* of a single chickadee scolding me from across the bog, the mad yelping of a few chained dogs beyond the upper rim of the hole and—with a distinctness never heard in summer—the roar of distant, diminished traffic.

Shortly after Christmas the first hard freeze of the season set in, as temperatures dipped below ten degrees at night and rose not much above twenty by day. One bright cold day at noon, with the temperature hovering at fifteen, I shuffled down to the bog. It had been glazed over smoothly by the preceding night's frost but was not yet safe to walk on. The new ice, though grooved to the touch with running, intersecting lines and needle-thin columns of bubbles, was clear and transparent. In places large, flattened white air bubbles, six inches and more across, lay just beneath the ice surface like giant fish scales. Bending down at the bog's edge, I was surprised to see that the water under the ice was visibly alive with hundreds of small, moving creatures—mostly daphnia, a group of tiny freshwater crustaceans—all rowing in short, jerky movements with feathered, leglike antennae. Prowling beneath them, a good deal larger but less clear to view, were what I took to be the voracious, elongated forms of dragonfly larvae.

I stepped gingerly out onto a small rock that protruded from the ice a few feet from shore to better watch these small submarine creatures jerking about in seemingly random directions, more like mechanical toys than fluid organisms, against a clear bottom of maple and oak leaves that were not noticeably decayed since they fell a few months ago.

I heard a rushing, soughing noise and looked up the western slope of the kettle hole to its crest, where, above the gray waste of oaks, a small stand of pitch pines swayed with stiff dignity in the slow wind. Large, individual clouds rolled up ponderously over the ridge of pines and shelved off stately to the south, peeling one by one across the face of the sun, which, from where I stood, shone just above the horizon: an Arctic noon. It was then that I decided to come back at night, after the ice had had a chance to freeze more solidly, to do a further exploration of this winter underworld.

About 10:30 that evening, under a cold, hard, gibbous moon, I carried a sackful of wood down into the hole and built a small fire in a cleared space at the edge of the bog. The steep-sided hollow yawned under the bright moonlight, and the twisted, heavy, dark limbs of the bordering swamp maples curled out over the ice like massive vines. Except that it was night, the weather was almost unchanged from earlier in the day. A light northwest wind still carded itself through the stiff brushes of the pines on the ridge, though when I lit my small bonfire (more as a source of light than of heat), the flames streamed toward me from the south—a reversal of winds common in kettle holes like this. The large clouds still rolled, one by one, along the ridge in solemn parade, clouds with dark centers and bushy, luminous, silver-gray edges, like the hollow, faceless busts of gods, engulfing and releasing the moon as they passed in succession.

The fire sprang up in a gust, throwing the bare limbs and shrubs into sudden relief: blueberry bushes hanging their sad heads out onto the bog ice, beech trees up the slope flinging their stiff branches upward in hysterical, frozen frenzy, like a tableau of keening women.

The warm, reddish glow of the fire seemed strange, possessing not only a different intensity from the moonlight but also a different quality of light that enclosed me in a bubble of color afloat in the surrounding silvered sea. I seemed to see with two sets of vision at once, a technicolor scene within a black-and-white movie. I was in Oz, moving through a sleeping Kansas.

Testing the ice, I found that it bore my weight without cracking, though I could still sense resilience in it. I took my flashlight and began exploring the perimeter of the bog on my hands and knees. The ice remained clear, even clearer in the penetrating beam of the flashlight and more alive than it had appeared during the day. The daphnia were still there, jerking along just under the surface in their pedestrian manner, but now they were accompanied by several other creatures. A large, black diving beetle, nearly an inch long, floated slowly up from the bottom, seemed to inhale some air from one of the bubbles caught under the ice, and darted down to the bottom again. A small, round, red water mite scurried along the bottom like a purposeful balloon.

There were also large numbers of what I had earlier mistaken for dragonfly larvae. Now I could see they were elongated, transparent organisms about three-quarters of an inch long, resembling large bilateral diatoms, but definitely animal. Each had two knobby protuberances containing what looked like eyespots near its front end. I guessed they were some sort of flatworm or insect larvae, but I had never seen anything like them before. There were several spots where dozens of them floated, motionless, just below the ice, looking in fact like so many slivers of ice. Every now and then one would move in a spasmodic manner, twisting its body into a crossed loop and then uncurling with a snap, a movement that shot it several inches in one direction. This seemed to be their only method of locomotion, and since it appeared quite random and undirected, it was probably a predator-escape reaction. Beneath these strange, jerking creatures there occasionally swam some large, black shapes several inches long (unmetamorphosed frog tadpoles?) moving in this miniature sea like the huge, submerged shapes of whales.

Most numerous of all, however, were squirming masses of a common, threadlike roundworm, reddish in color and about three inches long. I recognized them from last spring, when they had appeared in the bottom debris of the bog water of my aquarium. Now they had come out at night in winter and lay sprawled across the leaf floor of the bog, wriggling along under the ice.

It was an odd sight to see that many cold-blooded, soft-bodied invertebrates moving about briskly on the other side of this glass floor of ice, in water that could not have been much above freezing. They seemed so vulnerable there, so close to death. One of the worms, in fact, had come more than close. One end of its round, coral-colored body had become trapped in the ice above it, held stiff and unyielding while the rest of it writhed and thrashed about violently, even as the crystalizing ice continued to engulf it further. On my knees I watched, helpless to help, as the worm continued its futile, spasmodic jerkings and the ice fingers increased their grip, slowly embalming it like some minute, kettle-hole mammoth.

As I crawled about the bog, I found that my movements were creating downward water pressures that threw up clouds of debris and leaves from the bottom and sent the bog creatures scurrying and shimmering off in the dark currents. I flopped over on my back and lay spread out on the ice, a large, irregular island on its surface, while overhead the moon sliced its way through loamy, soiled clouds like a harrow disc. There was no animal sound at all, no owl, no dog. The breeze still soughed in the pines, but beyond it I heard, or thought I heard, another sound—a fainter, pulsing, insistent sound. In summer it might have been the roar of tourist traffic, muffled and softened by the sea of leaves in the hole. But now, in midwinter, traveling in over an iron landscape, it was too diffuse and constant to be the sound of cars. It seemed to emanate from the earth itself, a sound more felt than heard, as though its vibrations reverberated beneath me on the bog's ice. And then I recognized what it was . . .

Slowly I got up and returned to the fire, which had died down, sucking all the color back out of the night with it. With my boots I scattered the glowing brands out onto the ice, where they hissed and slithered like serpents. Then I turned and climbed back up out of the silver bowl, toward the dark outline of the house that lay, huge and silent, like some brooding leviathan on the crest of the hill:

Oh, it is a marvelous night now. The house sits stiff and unmoving in a wind that pours in from the Bay with increased strength, making the oaks swing and creak in their frozen sockets. The yard sparkles with frost under the high moon, whose light possesses the sky now, drowning out all but the brightest stars. I stand and listen again, to be sure. Down in the dark bog the ice creaks loudly, as though recovering from my weight. Then I hear it again, more definite now, yes: the sound of surf. From a mile away it rumbles in from the north, carried in from the Bay on the wind across beach and marsh, up the creviced slopes of the moraine, over the cedar-studded mound of Red Top Cemetery shining under the moon like some white, rounded dune, and into my yard.

I live well inland, on a ridge that is likely to be safe from ocean storms for the the next five thousand years or more. Yet the low, heavy sound of distant swells whispers, tells me that there is no true inland to this peninsula. Now, in winter, when the land lies open and exposed, we can perceive that its essential character is in its endless tug-of-war, its penetrating and unresolved marriage with the sea. Our shores lie at the edge of perpetual watery wilderness, one that does not wait, like the forest, for us to enter and conquer, but that itself rises to nibble and gouge away at our foundations, overwashing our beaches and marshes, invading our roads, our village streets, our very backyards.

Even here, deep in the wooded folds of the moraine, I feel the sea wind and hear the rushing surf. I sense the running alewives, the humping, hissing seals, the scuttling crabs, the buried and ice-crushed life of the flats, the coursing sea turtles and pulsing squid, and the young, leaping sea birds—all sea-bred, sea-loving creatures, caught in their rush to meet the oncoming waves, even as the planet itslf rushes on through cold space, breasting the solar winds. In the sound of the surf is their break and dash from cover across naked sands, their wide roamings, many deaths, and the casting of innumerable spat, eggs, calves, and pups into the ocean's gravid currents.

CHAPTER 8

The Uses of Alewives

1

Each year, in May, when I go to our annual town meeting and look over the official warrant, I find, tucked among zoning amendments, road repairs, and requests for new police cruisers, a short article that asks, "To see what action the Town will take with regard to its Herring or Alewife fisheries." And each year, along with the rest of the assembled citizens of Brewster, I vote "that the fishing rights at Stony Brook Herring Run not be sold."

The herring-rights question is hardly one of the more momentous articles on the town's multimillion-dollar budget. It is barely given a glance by the finance committee or the board of selectmen, for it is not likely to affect the tax rate, property values, and the health and safety of the community, or to cause neighbor to rise up against neighbor. It has, rather, become one of the "fixtures" at town meeting, along with articles to give the dog tax to the Brewster Ladies Library or to contribute annually to the pension of a retired teacher now living near Boston. Like these, it receives almost automatic approval, provoking no controversy and little discussion, except every now and then when a new resident rises to ask what in the world an "alewife" is.

The local "herrin'," or alewife—*Alosa pseudoharengus*—is a member of the herring family, which includes shad, menhaden, and the more familiar sea or "sardine" herring. About a foot in length, it is a large-eyed, small-mouthed, silvery-scaled fish with a deep belly and a row of sharp serrations on its ventral ridge that have given it the name of "sawbelly" in some localities. Its more common name of "alewife" is said to derive from a loose association of its pronounced abdomen with the alewives or female tavern keepers of Elizabethan England, who were traditionally represented as large-bellied women.

The alewife is an anadromous fish; that is, like the salmon, it makes an annual spring migration from its saltwater home up coastal rivers and streams to spawn in freshwater ponds and lakes. Beginning with a trickle of individuals and small groups in March, their yearly journey, or run, swells to a flood of millions upon millions of fish by late April or early May, as the alewives enter the small brooks and larger estuaries all along the New England coast, pushing upstream to cast their milt and roe (as the sperm and eggs are termed) along the shores of protected ponds and quiet backwaters.

Unlike the larger salmon, however, most alewives do not die after spawning, at least not in the shorter runs. Instead, they return to the ocean, where they may travel hundreds of miles during the winter before returning to their home stream once again the following spring. The eggs, left to hatch by themselves, develop into small herring fry, and about a month after the adults have left, the little alewives, barely two inches long, yield to the current and are swept seaward also. There, a small percentage will survive and, in three or four years, using some chemical identification system still poorly understood, will themselves return to spawn in the waters where they were born.

Brewster's herring article goes back at least to the early part of this century, when the "rights" to the run were traditionally sold each spring to the highest commercial bidder. This was frequently an off-Cape fish wholesaler who would come and net hundreds of barrels of alewives out of the large seining pool just above Stony Brook Road in order to sell them for lobster bait or fish meal. The practice ceased in the early 1960s, due as much, I suspect, to a decline in the run's economic importance as to any heightening of environmental sensitivity. Still, the article has remained on the warrant, and every year since then the town has dutifully voted "not to sell the rights" to its alewives, though no one any longer comes to make an offer.

Not only has the herring article lost its pragmatic purpose; it no longer makes even calendar sense. It used to be considered when the annual meetings were held in early March, before the fish had begun to come in in any numbers. Now that the meeting date has been pushed forward to May, to better correspond with the state's fiscal year, action is not taken until the better part of the run is already over. This is something like waiting until the Fourth of July to decide you will not plant peas.

A cynic might suggest that the article's very lack of significance makes it appropriate for our town meetings, which to many minds have become an increasingly anachronistic and empty form of local government whose functions have been largely usurped by state and federal mandates. One might argue that the value of the herring-rights article today lies less in affording any protection to the fish than in helping to provide newcomers with the illusion that they have moved, not into the largely suburban retirement community that Brewster is rapidly becoming, but into a quaint Cape Cod village with quirky little fish articles on its warrant.

Yet there is a certain enthusiasm in the chorus of "Ayes" that yearly greets the question, a genuine note of endorsement that suggests perhaps the alewives are still of some use to us, as they once were, though in ways less easy to measure than a dollar-and-cents bid. On the other hand, perhaps we are merely grateful for a short breather from the thornier budget items on the warrant, from ever-increasing municipal costs and the pressures of growth, from the bitter feelings and divisiveness that frequently accompany these small-town gatherings. Amid a sense of diminishing home rule and the lack of any common vision for our future, we may well feel gratitude for the chance to give heartfelt, unanimous approval to something, to say, "We stand for fish"—if not much else.

2
———

It was not always so. Alewives once played a vital and central role in local affairs, and the many "Herring Rivers" that thread their way into the sandy fabric of the Cape's shoreline have exerted a powerful influence on local patterns of human settlement, and in our town more than in most.

The herring run at Stony Brook in West Brewster, about a mile east of my house, is one of the largest and healthiest runs on Cape Cod, primarily because of the abundance of suitable breeding habitat found in the string of six or seven ponds lying above its headwaters. It has been estimated that in good years over half a million fish come in from the Bay to swim up the stream's winding mile-and-a-half course. The alewives of Stony Brook have been returning to this small watercourse for thousands of years, and there is evidence that human beings have been involved in their comings and goings for much, if not most, of that time.

Over the years a great number of Indian artifacts have been collected along the banks and hilly slopes of Stony Brook Valley; most of them have ended up in the archaeological repository of the Cape Cod Museum of Natural History. The sheer bulk of stone axes, broken hammer stones, flakes, and other objects points to a long and continued use of the area by local prehistoric peoples. Some, such as certain stone spear points designed for catching fish, suggest the presence of a halieutic Indian culture in the valley as much as 7,000 years ago. The tribes there at the time of the first European settlers were known as the Saquatuckets. They died off before any direct account was made of their manner of living, but from what we know of other contemporary coastal cultures it seems likely that they set up camp at the base of the western hills in order to receive the morning sun, wove nets out of rushes growing along the banks, set them across the stream to trap the surging tides of migrating herring in spring, and built fires to smoke their catch for future use.

Today most alewives are taken from the fish ladder at the head of the valley, over a mile inland from the Bay, where Stony Brook Road crosses the stream from which it received its name. The present ladder consists of a series of small concrete locks and pools built in 1948, but the first white inhabitants of Brewster settled at this same spot over 300 years ago. Like the Indians before them, these early colonists were drawn in part by the reliable and easily harvested seasonal food supply that the alewives represented.

But in a land short on running waters, such modest streams as Stony Brook were valued even more as a source of power. In 1661 Gov. Thomas Prence of the Old Colony built the town's first gristmill, on the east side of the brook, just below the road. Not long afterward a fulling mill was constructed above the road, and as the little settlement prospered, more buildings and enterprises grew up along the stream banks: a woolen mill, a tannery, a stage coach inn, a district school, a stove works, and a shoe factory.

By the early nineteenth century Stony Brook supported a thriving commercial community that had acquired its own name of Factory Village. It continued to prosper until just after the Civil War, when a decline in the merchant-marine fleet and a general exodus from New England to the newly opened farmlands of the Midwest spelled economic disaster for most of Cape Cod. The old mills were abandoned, and in subsequent decades several of them burned, including the original seventeenth-century gristmill in 1871. The other industries failed or moved off the Cape, and many of the old houses became derelict or, like the schoolhouse, were moved to other locations to serve other purposes. In 1873 a new gristmill was built on the site of the old fulling mill; there it continued to grind corn, and later to churn ice cream, until 1940, when it was finally purchased by the town. Today it still grinds corn for tourists at twenty-five cents a bag, with recipes for corn muffins and a generous amount of local history thrown in free by Winslow Dunnells, a descendant of Brewster's original miller.

The center of town as well as the earnestness of human endeavor that was once concentrated here have long since shifted away from Stony Brook, though the herring themselves continue to come in no less earnestly. Alewives continued to provide an important seasonal food supply for local inhabitants well into this century. Charlie Ellis remembers having "herrin' " for breakfast often as a boy, and he once told me a story about a girl in his grammar school named Avis— "Avis, that was what they called her"—who was late to class one day. When the teacher asked her why she was so late, she replied, "Well, m'am, we had herrin' this morning and it took me a time to get all the bones out of my mouth."

Though many residents today still smoke and pickle alewives, sauté their roe, or use the fish for bait and fertilizer, they are no longer regarded as the vital local resource they once were. Their economic value now is primarily as a spring tourist attraction, something to take up the slack before The Season arrives.

Yet if their commercial importance has declined, alewives have been increasingly recognized as an important component and link in a broad chain of aquatic environments. In the ocean the adult fish feed several species of game and commercial saltwater species. As they journey upstream to the spawning ponds, alewives are easy prey for the hundreds of gulls that line the banks and with sharp beaks rip the milt and roe sacs out of the still-living fish. After the gulls' depredation, bloody carcasses line the stream banks and bottom, supplying food for numerous land and water organisms, from skunks and muskrats to bacterial decomposers. Once in the ponds, the adults are relatively safe from predators, but the astronomical numbers of eggs and fry provide abundant forage for perch, bass, pickerel, white suckers, frogs, snakes, turtles, and other freshwater wildlife. And when the young, minnow-sized herring begin to follow the adults downstream in late summer, they are snapped up by the thousands by eels, herons, and other denizens of the marsh and estuarine systems. Few creatures, in fact, are used so well by so many others and in so many forms. Alewives are one of the great common coins of the natural realm.

Recently a new function of the alewives' migration has been recognized, one that may serve to endear them even more to an energy-conscious age. A current state guide to coastal wetlands points out that their "unique spawning migrations are of added significance because they permit the direct transfer of energy from the marine food web to estuarine, freshwater and terrestrial ecosystems." In other words, their upstream journeys may be taken as blows against entropy, a gesture of life against the downstream and dissipating currents of the inanimate universe.

The first Puritan settlers, of course, knew nothing about the second law of thermodynamics or the complexities of aquatic food chains. Yet ever since the enactment of Plymouth Colony Fish Law in 1623—the first "wildlife legislation" in New England—official protection and passage have been provided for these fish. Stony Brook has ever been, first, last, and always, a "herrin' river," and throughout its long history, spanning thousands of years of human use, industry, change, and abandonment, the alewives have continued to run with a humbling and impersonal consistency. Perhaps, in their journeys, they may still offer us grist and nourishment for our lives.

3
———

One morning in early March I drove down to the run to see whether any fish had come in. I did not really expect to find any yet, though alewives have been known to arrive in streams on the south shore of the Cape as early as the second week in February.

The water flowing through the concrete locks of the fish ladder was still icy green and savage looking, turbid, high, and muddy from the silt and salt and slush washing down off the road into the series of pools below. The stream banks were lined with the wreckage of winter—torn grapevines, loosened rocks, boards, cans, and cartons. The road crews would not arrive for several weeks yet to clean up the area for the spring tourists.

It was not cosmetics, however, that held back the fish but the water itself. The rule of thumb regarding alewives is that they will begin to migrate upstream when the temperature of the outflowing waters exceeds that of the estuary or bay into which they empty. In Cape Cod Bay this normally occurs around the time of the vernal equinox, but last winter was one of the coldest on record, and the millponds above Stony Brook had only recently begun to break up from their long freeze. Thin crescents of ice could still be seen retreating into their western coves, and fragments of old snow crumbled along the shores among the ruins of last year's sedges. Though a few chickadees were already practicing their clear-whistled mating calls in the bare maples overhead, Stony Brook continued to run with the cold currents of denial, empty of fish.

For the next few weeks I continued to stop at the run every other day or so. By mid-March the red-maple buds had cracked their thin shells, sending pale pink, filamentous pistils out into the raw air. The long, yellowing branches of the bankside willows swayed enticingly over the swirling, cloudy waters of the run. But still the fish ladder pools remained empty, as empty as the local baseball fields, tennis courts, town landings, backyard gardens, and other sites of spring rituals yet to come.

By the third week of the month, alewives were being caught in gill nets just offshore and there were reports of a few fish having been sighted up at the run in the Cape Cod Canal. It was not until March 28, however, that I finally saw my first herring of the season. It was a single fish, swimming alone in the last pool below the road—a fleet, elusive form, blue-gray and brown finned in the water. As always, there was a sense of joyful recognition in seeing the familiar form and its movement in the brook. It represented more than itself, more even than its race; it was a sign that all was still well in the world from which it had come.

But there was something odd about this fish: it was alone. Alewives exist in the plural, and it is difficult to think of them otherwise, except as some dead specimen, removed and on display. To see one alewife by itself is like watching a maple tree bear a single leaf, or one bee keeping a hive, or a lone wave beating toward shore.

Its motion was also strange. It seemed to sense its aloneness. The fish would swim upstream the length of the pool and then, instead of leaping up through the foot-high lock to the next pool, it would circle back with baffled, uncertain movements to the lower end of the pool where it had begun. From there it would swim forward again—only to become lost once more and slowly circle back.

Again and again the lone alewife made its pass, and each time, when it reached the rushing tongue of water that poured through the lock from the next pool, it balked and returned to its starting point. Many things might have been holding it back: too strong a flow of water, some obstruction at the lock that I couldn't see, or just some necessary waiting period before it would be prepared to leap up to the next level. Yet there seemed something more, something in the fish's own movements that didn't feel right to itself. It was as though it missed the accompanying motion of those who were not there yet, as though it were trying, by circling back, to pick up its absent companions. Where, it seemed to ask by its repeated forward thrusts, were the press and momentum, the blossom, buzz, and roar of the completing crowd?

4

The herring began running in earnest during the second week in April, just about the same time that candidates did in the upcoming municipal elections. The latter tend to congregate at such traditional politicking spots as the general store, the town dump, and the post office, shaking hands and trying to garner votes. As far as I know, however, no local politician has ever tried running at the herring run, though during April it is *the* gathering place in town.

When I stop at the fish ladder now, I always find several cars parked there. The question on everyone's lips is constantly the same—"Are they running yet?" A week ago I still had to look carefully to see fish; now I see them without looking. They swarm and weave by the dozens beneath the scrim of flashing waters and rippled shadows, like dark beads strung on the flowing, twisting necklace of the stream. The yellow leaves of the overhanging willows have slipped out like thin tongues, and the white blossoms of the shadbush, named for a cousin of the alewife that also migrates at this time, shed their petals into the stream.

One morning shortly after Easter, the gulls woke me with their cries and screams. Though nearly a mile away, their strident cacophony carried clearly, letting me know that the alewives were there in force now. As I drove down Stony Brook Road, I saw scores of white bodies soaring high above the run, circling and beating their wings in the first rays of dawn like signal flags run up an invisible pole.

When I arrived, a little after six, a light, cold wind was running up the valley. The sky was clear and alight with day, but the sun itself remained hidden behind the low glacial hills that rose abruptly to the east, giving a shadowed, late-afternoon feeling to the area around the mill.

The scene was like something out of Hitchcock's *The Birds:* gulls were perched everywhere, on the cedar railings bordering the road, in trees overhanging the run, crowded onto the rocks in the pond narrows just above the fish ladder, strolling along the rock walls, and even in the street. They were lined up in rows along the roof ridges of the mill, and the old stagecoach inn and other older houses about the run, as well as on several of the more recently built houses overlooking the valley—defecating democratically on old and new alike.

I estimated some four to five hundred gulls in the immediate vicinity, no more, perhaps, than can be seen around the run on any good day. But when the human crowds are here, the mass of gulls tend to keep their distance, as they do at the dump. Now they seemed to occupy our streets, our houses, and our yards with unchallenged possession, as a dominant presence.

Farther downstream, hidden from view, I could hear a swarm of the birds descending on the fish in the water. But the gulls around the mill for the most part sat nervously quiet in the shade of dawn's unreleased light, chucking, coughing, and mewing with restrained anticipation, like the fuse to some hidden explosive, quietly sizzling. Their contained appearance—cold, red eyes, cream white heads, and neat, handsome, ash gray coats—added to the eerie feeling of calm about to burst with violence.

Then I saw I was not alone. Two older men in hip boots were struggling up to the road from the lower ladder, carrying between them a plastic garbage can full of herring that they had gathered with nets. Technically, the two men had been breaking the law by gathering the fish before sunrise. But the overwhelming presence of the gulls seemed to suspend human law, and now they both stood near me, looking in a kind of bemused awe at the cordon of gulls surrounding us. One motioned with his head to the mass of birds lined up along the ridge of the old stagecoach inn across the road.

"Be hard to sleep in there," he offered.

We spoke casually, but in instinctively hushed tones, until finally a newspaper truck swept down the hill between us and the gulls, and the pair got into their car and left.

I walked down beside the lower pools and saw that the gulls had indeed had a night, or early dawn, of it. Everywhere lay strewn the bodies of alewives, some half-eaten, some untouched, but most with their abdomens ripped out where the gulls had searched for roe, a delicacy with them as with us. A few fish, their bodies sliced open, were still flapping weakly in the foot-worn dust beside the ladder; I pushed them back into the water with my feet.

The fish ladder was full of living, straining bodies, rising in the boiling pools in curved, flat flashes of dark green, silver, pink, and yellow, almost as though someone were pushing them up from below. But the constant, close presence of the gulls made me almost unaware of the fish. The muddy banks were covered with their overlapping, crossbow tracks. As I walked down below the pools, the gulls merely sidled out of my way or fluttered off a foot or two. They seemed to know that this was still their hour, that territory is a matter of time as well as space, and though the scale of day was tilting further toward me with each passing moment, it still came down on their side.

On the surface, at least, their savagery, waste, and gluttony, as well as their peremptory air, was hardly different from that of the crowds of people that would be here in a few hours, squeezing the fish roughly to see whether they contained milt or roe, then throwing the bruised males back, hemorrhaged, perhaps, or mortally sprained. What appropriate companions these gulls are for us! What outward beauty!

Continuing a little farther downstream, however, I found that the gulls themselves did not escape mortality here. At the second bend, in a quiet backwater pool, I came upon two of their bodies, rocking gently in the back eddies of the stream as though asleep, their heads turned away and trailing down into the water. Theirs seemed a much more peaceful death than that of the gulls who smashed forms commonly line our beaches in winter. In the moving stream the herring, sparkling with the iridescence of the abiding seas from which they came, nosed past the gray and white floating bodies, running silently on toward the torrent of the ladder and the still, scented ponds that lay beyond.

5

During the last week in April, the run is at its peak. So many fish are in the ladder that they cover the surface of the pools like dark moving blankets. Clouds of gulls fill the valley, wheeling slowly over the old Factory Village site and spreading themselves out by the hundreds along the broad salt marshes that border the lower reaches of the stream.

Now the people are drawn here in numbers commensurate with those of the alewives. The meager parking area quickly overflows. The sides of Stony Brook Road are choked with cars, pickup trucks, bicycles, and school and tourist buses from all over New England. The town has hired a policeman to direct traffic and oversee the taking of fish; but as he frantically waves his arms in the middle of the road, he appears to be a man drowning in cars and bodies. During the week, men and women with nets and large plastic buckets come to gather fish for bait, for smoking and salting, or for no reason at all, simply because there is such an abundance for the taking. Though no fish are allowed to be taken from Friday through Sunday, the crowds then are even larger. Small children with weekend fathers perch on the rocks and concrete locks, grappling the fish with their hands and throwing them from one pool to another. One small boy of about five approaches the policeman and asks him whether he can have a dead fish for his cat.

"Dead?" the officer replies, looking perplexed. "There aren't supposed to be any."

If the run is a place for rediscovering ties to the past, it is equally a place for renewing present acquaintances and making new ones. It is one of those spontaneous seasonal meeting places—like the clam flats, the eel ponds, and the crab creeks—that draw us for reasons other than mere sociability, but where we become more social out of common need or desire or simply mutual curiosity.

For some of the local residents, it is a scene they have repeated each year since they were small. For others, immigrants like myself, it can be a way of creating identity, of borrowing a sense of history we were not born to. For the children, native or imported, it is simply plain, unalloyed, and sometimes brutal entertainment.

There is one woman I know who, for fifty years, has driven the same Model A Ford over to the Stony Brook run each spring to get alewives for a long and unbroken line of house cats. "One herrin'," she claims, "will straighten out a summer case of cat rickets." She keeps a freezer full of fish through the year but has given her neighbors instructions, in case of her sudden death, to get rid of them immediately: "I don't want folks to say, 'Poor Elmira, she had to live on herrin'.' "

One day I found a truck from the state Department of Fisheries and Game parked beside the run, its three-man crew busily loading fish from the stream into a large, open fiberglass tank that sat on the truck bed. Stony Brook, being one of the largest herring runs in Massachusetts, is frequently used by the Commonwealth to replenish existing runs or stock new ones in other towns. This load, I was told, was marked for one in Yarmouthport, two towns away.

The tank was about seven feet long, three feet wide, and three feet deep, and had two gasoline-motor pumps mounted beside it. The youngest of the three men was down in the first pool below the road, scooping out fish with a long-handled net. He carried each netful to the second man, standing beside the truck, who in turn handed them up to the third man, standing on the truck bed, who finally dumped them into the open tank.

The man on the truck invited me to come up and watch the operation. The tank was divided into three compartments and was initially filled by one of the pumps through a long, green hose going down into the stream. That pump was off now, and the second one was circulating the water, aerating it and shooting it back into the tank through several plastic jets strapped to the sides a few inches above the water level—a sort of herring Jacuzzi. The fish boiled and thrashed in their confined waters as in the tumbling pools below, like salmon in foaming rapids, a caldron of alewives all gray-green above and silver-pink below. I was told that the tank held about 1,500 fish, which were delivered with "very little mortality."

Leaving the men to their work, I walked down below the fish ladder and out onto the wooden bridge that spans the lower end of the run. There I was joined by a young woman who had come down from Boston. She said she had heard on Channel 5 that the alewives were in, so she drove down to see them, "as shown on TV." She remarked that the ones down here by the bridge looked smaller than those in the pools above. I suggested it might be the effect of the wider context here, of the fish not being so crowded, as the moon seems to shrink as it rises into a wider sky. They reminded her, she said, of the Southeast Expressway.

Yet though crowded fin to fin, the herring never jostle one another awkwardly as human crowds and traffic do. Though each fish seems possessed with an urgent energy, they bear their heavy numbers with a surpassing grace and ability, circling and waiting with settled tension for their chance to leap, as though shot from a sling, up through each pouring tongue of water. In that fluid regimentation their pink, scaly backs gleam fresh and new and clean with each jump through the dark, tumbling water. Their progression seems to have the overtones of a stately, formal dance.

I had gone down to the run that day to collect a few dozen herring to put beneath my hills of corn, in the old Indian fashion. When I first came here, I used to take live fish. To shorten their suffering I would take each herring in one hand and crack its skull with a hammer blow, feeling the shiver of its life run down its backbone and out through its tail. Each year, however, it grew harder and harder for me to do this. I seemed to shut off half of my mind in the process, dealing the death-blows obliquely, so to speak, though in some strange way this only increased my awareness of what I was doing.

This was no squeamishness on my part, no tenderer-than-thou attitude toward killing. The fish, I knew, suffered crueler treatment than mine from nature. Part of it, I suppose, was a growing reluctance to take anything when the passion of its life was upon it; having come so far in their risk-spiked journey, the fish seemed to deserve better than to be taken a few hundred feet from their goal merely to end up in a corn patch.

In any case, it soon became obvious that such taking of life was unnecessary. A dead alewife will grow corn as well as a live one, and despite the policeman's disclaimer, there are always plenty of fish carcasses lying about at the height of the run. One of the best places to find them is at the base of the small rocky falls near the wooden bridge, where a diverted side stream plummets some six feet to rejoin the main brook. A dozen or more dead or dying fish are usually here, having thrashed themselves to exhaustion in futile attempts to scale such an impossible height. They lie limply in the shallows, belly up, or wedged tightly among the rocks at the base. One day I gathered nearly thirty dead fish in this small area, and I was struck by the contrast between the pale, flat appearance of the recently dead bodies and the varied shining hues on the living forms being netted in the upper pools. This seemed to consist mostly in the rapid loss of iridescent pink along the upper sides of the dead alewives.

Several of the fish at the base of the falls were still alive. I pried one loose from between two rocks and threw it back into the deeper stream below, where it slowly righted itself, remaining slightly listed, and then tried, limply, to work its way back up to the falls. I soon realized that such efforts were futile, much like trying to push beached whales offshore. These herring have a collective mind and intention of their own, an inner direction that, however wasteful and pointless some aspects of it might seem to me, was nonetheless an integral part of the species' overall strategy of survival.

Besides, there is something about the bloody, undisguised candor and natural appetite of this place that I relish and that seems to excite raw emotion and primitive response in the midst of this pastoral setting, as though the alewives brought in with them something of the sea's own violence. As I harvested the dead herring below the fish ladder, the people in the upper pools continued to move and press beside the stream, nets and buckets in hand, jockeying for position, while the children, straining to see as they stood on rocks beside the pools, screamed with surprise and delight.

There is, of course, a strong element of cruelty in children and their enthusiasms. I have seen alewives used as baseball bats, or tossed over the mill wheel to crash on the rocks below, or left alive on the banks, like discarded toys, gasping and dust covered, to thrash and die. Such practices have led many people in town to suggest putting a chain-link fence around the entire area, as has been done at some other runs. Yet despite the abuse and misuse, I cannot help feeling that there is something salutary, overall, about such close and unfettered contact. The fish arrive to us already scarred and gashed by the gratuitous savagery of the gulls that swarm further downstream. Perhaps by netting, grasping, squeezing, and bludgeoning them, we too may catch something of the fish's own fire, passed on to us by the gulls, passing on upstream, like some watery torch.

The alternative—sanitary observation—does not seem much better. Too many times I have seen schoolchildren marched through national parks and wildlife refuges in hushed reverence, in order to produce beautiful, informed tidbits about Nature. This strikes me as just the way to teach them that the natural world is something to be visited, appreciated, and preserved, like some valuable historic relic, rather than wantonly devoured, as it should be at their age. I myself have given talks here to school groups for the natural history museum, and I find that the hardest part is having to stress to the children that they should not handle the fish unnecessarily. This is important, I know, since handling them removes some of the protective oily coating on their scales, exposing them to injury and a type of fungus disease. Nonetheless, I do not like my role as stifler, even in the name of conservation. What I say goes against their deepest impulses. What the children want—what *I* want—is not to learn about the fish but to *join* them. Life demands participation. What we need is not kid gloves, in approved wrappings, but kids' eyes, sharp new eyes to pierce another layer of the mystery. At any rate, we are born wet and are in too far to stay dry.

As we gathered the fish, live ones and dead ones, the shad-blossom petals fell one by one into the water, mixing with the clumps of silver scales shed by the herring in their passage upstream. Strands of willow leaves waved like kelp in the air, throwing a soft, yellow-green veil over the harsh elements of struggle and violence. Through the branches of maples and willows, the obscured and atavistic shapes of the gulls wove and cut as through a morning fog, while beside the road the transfer of fish continued into the fiberglass tank on the state truck, chugging away like some motorized plasma bag siphoning off its pint of blood.

6

One evening in mid-May, after a particularly long and contentious town meeting, I stopped at the run on my way home to clear my mind and let some of the accumulated heat dissipate in the dark, roiling waters of the stream. Though these meetings still seem to me the best of many imperfect forms of local self-government, they frequently engender a good deal of hard feelings. It is impossible, in such gatherings, not to take certain statements or votes personally. We are not polished politicians, jousting at one another in traditional, mutually understood, stylized forms of attack or aggression; rather, we are neighbors and amateur, part-time democrats who tend to speak what we feel. We can at one moment be meanly selfish, denying water mains or street lights to one part of town because it is not "in the public interest," and, in the next second, be conventionally responsible about "property rights" and "progress," meekly accepting those outside forces that continue to transform and dictate the destiny of our town, resigned to what we all stand most to lose by. No wonder we look for small, unimportant articles to worry over—herring rights, a new water cooler for the town hall, "historically appropriate" paint colors for our houses—like dogs fighting over old bones in some back alley.

At the run, business was proceeding as usual. The alewives were still there in full numbers, black and shining in the pools of light cast by the streetlamp across the road. They appeared larger at night for some reason, and the brook itself seemed abnormally full, overflowing the tops of the locks and splashing up onto the banks, as though the great mass of fish in its waters had actually displaced their own medium and raised the level of the stream.

But the fish themselves seemed calmer now, strangely subdued (I am tempted to say "cool and collected"), though their ranks were not as strictly ordered, nor were individuals as strongly oriented to the current, as they were by day. Gulls do not generally feed on them at night, so that perhaps they sensed a certain lack of threat under cover of darkness and relaxed, or at least slackened a bit.

There now also appeared to be as many fish falling back down the ladder as going up. This is about the time when the two flows begin to overlap, those that have spawned and those that have yet to reach their goal. At night it was difficult to tell the spent from the unspent, for both those still going up through the locks and those coming down remain oriented upstream, toward the current.

I knelt beside the pool just below the road and tried to follow the movement of one fish, but it was impossible to do so for more than a few seconds. They were constantly encountering one another, yet managed to move smoothly together, with no jarring bumps, no clumsy encounters, no hard feelings. They seemed to say there is always an appeal to nature from human anxiety.

I found that by putting my hand slowly in the water among them I could actually pet them, letting them flow and curl under the touch of my fingers. By being very careful and unhurried I eventually managed to take hold of one fish without panicking it, gradually closing my grip around its slippery form so that it may have seemed to the alewife only the gradual tightening of the current about its torso.

I lifted the alewife gently out of the water and into the light of the streetlamp: a wet, scaly, glistening fistful. *Well, fish, what do you think of the night air?* By way of an answer, it thrashed violently with a whiplike snap several times, then lay quiet and limp in my palm. When I placed it back into the water, it released its panic suddenly, shooting violently straight across the pool and partway up the opposite bank two or three times before finally falling back and joining the slowly swarming crowd.

These night fish seem to be my own thoughts, racing along or dropping back with motivations and intentions of their own, forming shifting momentary patterns, leaping and fragmenting in the dark, pouring tongues of water and then coming together again on the next level in new shapes, new designs.

In the pools they wait, swimming without advancing in the fast current, having the power, as Frost says, of standing still "in the rush of everything to waste." They are my darker thoughts, running counter to time, counter to the current flow of ideas, displacing time itself, straining their man-made confines until there is more fish than stream, more thought than time. I come to the run to collect them by day, at appointed hours and in regulated amounts, but here in the dark they run on in uncounted numbers. They are potent, living, swimming forms—but not mine to claim until I can grasp them fully, utter them completely, until I fill my veins with their own running force.

Shining my flashlight in the pool, I saw the long, pale shape of an eel, nearly three feet in length, winding sinuously among the fish, which paid it no heed at all. Eels have a life cycle roughly opposite to that of the herring. They spawn in the ocean, return as young elvers to their parent streams in the spring, live in fresh water for four to six years, and then return in late summer or fall as mature adults to spawn in salt water, after which they die. What is this one doing here now? I wondered. Is it going up or down? Do these fish ever sleep? Does anyone know why they make these tortuous journeys, eels or alewives?

Each curling, black, finny shape seemed to be a dark question mark, and the eel's long, thick body underscored the depths of my ignorance about them all. Finally the eel looped away out of my beam of light into darkness, and the fish came on, or dropped back through the locks, knowing what they knew.

We have long fished in these waters, and though most of us now come primarily to look, it is as if we sense a continuing value in these anadromous herring that transcends any practical use we may once have found or may yet discover in them. Surely they provide us with the closest thing we have left to a natural celebration; the perennial gathering of families at the run each April and May to watch the resurgence and birth of life in Stony Brook is a kind of spontaneous community festival, all the more authentic for being unorganized and unofficial. It represents an unconscious acknowledgment of our own past, not only that recent past when we sold the fishing rights for cash, but further back when the run was central to the life of the town, and even more distantly to the time of the original Indian inhabitants who also gathered here in spring and whose artifacts still turn up along the banks of the stream.

In an age when most towns have lost what John Hay calls their "rooted continuity," the Stony Brook run represents an unbroken and vital tie with our beginnings. There is still a living memory stored in its currents, and in the fish that swim in them. Whether we gather them to eat, to bury in our gardens, or simply to feel in them the raw, cold power of the sea coursing through our inland veins, they remind us of our continued participation in and ultimate dependence upon the natural cycles and free passage of life upon this planet.

The real significance of the herring-rights article that appears on our town warrant each year may lie not in any direct material benefit we still receive from the fish but in the very persistence of our concern in the face of the run's diminishing practical importance. Such concern, at least, represents the closest we come in local politics to a pure recognition of the right of another species to coexist with us irrespective of whatever "use" it may or may not have. In the process I think we have gone far toward redefining the term *rights* itself. The herring rights we once so jealously guarded or cautiously bartered for our own gain have in recent years been increasingly transferred from us to the fish themselves. For all our increased knowledge of them, we are hard put to say exactly why we wish to protect these fish, what good they are to us, except perhaps that they have been with us so long that they now form part of our own local identity and that, like the lone alewife I watched swimming in the fish ladder back in March, we would feel incomplete without them.

Each spring, when we raise our collective voice at town meeting and vote "not to sell the rights to the herring run," we act better than we know, extending our suffrage to all life and serving as proxy for thousands of ancient members of our community who at that very moment are rushing in to meetings of their own on a full night tide.

CHAPTER 9

A Day on the Pond

1

By June most of the alewives in Stony Brook have reached their spawning grounds above the head of the stream in the string of connected waterbodies known collectively as the Mill Ponds. Unlike Berry's Hole and most of Brewster's other ponds, the Mill Ponds drain from one to the other and empty through the outlet at the head of the herring run. This modest flow has maintained the small openings, or "narrows," between the ponds that would otherwise have been closed off long ago by the natural buildup of silt barrier beaches.

The first in this chain of half a dozen or so ponds is Lower Mill Pond, a moderately large body of freshwater comprising some twenty-seven acres, studded with large glacial erratics that protrude from its waters near the shore, and ringed for the most part with low, heavily wooded hills that drop steeply down into the pond. In the summer its outflowing waters provide power for the town's gristmill, as they have done for over three centuries. Bordering the pond's eastern shore is a narrow, climbing, twisting road known as Run Hill Road. In the 1700s and early 1800s, it led to a large sheep common that existed in what is now an extensive wooded area south of the mill ponds. Later in the nineteenth century the road was a thoroughfare to a major cranberry industry in the same vicinity. Today it continues to carry heavy traffic along the pond's perimeter to the town dump, or "sanitary landfill," which is situated only a few hundred feet back from the pond shore, screened from view by stands of pitch pine along the eastern bluffs.

Lower Mill Pond is thus neither remote nor overlooked, and yet it is never crowded, not even on the hottest weekends in July, when most Cape Cod beaches resemble a state of siege and it is often difficult to find parking within a quarter mile of the Bay. Part of its relative neglect is due to its largely hilly shoreline and limited public access, but much of it lies in the nature of the pond itself. Lower Mill is a eutrophic pond, a scientific term that literally means "good growth." Its waters are shallow (thirteen feet is the maximum depth), warm, rich in plant nutrients and organic matter, and seasonally low in oxygen. Such ponds generally have little appeal for swimmers, and Lower Mill, though larger than many eutrophic ponds, is no exception.

Its low stretches of shoreline are overgrown with wild grass, cranberry vines, moss, scrub oak, pine saplings, and blueberry bushes, and they are frequently littered with goose turds and the carcasses of dead fish washed ashore. The vegetation does not stop at the pond's edge but steps unbroken down into the water itself, where it changes character, forming a thick fringe of rush and sedge along the shore and carpeting the pond bottom with oozy, submerged growth. The water tends to be murky in summer, filled with plant material and organic sediment, which make it a fine place for bottom scavengers of various phyla. Snapping turtles of prodigious size abound there, though I have never heard of any swimmer being bothered by one while in the water. (Disturbing a snapper on land is quite a different matter.) After wading in the shallows, though, one is likely to find two or three small, harmless leeches attached to the soles of one's feet.

The location of the shoreline itself is subject to great variation from season to season. This is partly due to natural fluctuations in water level, but in summer the condition is aggravated by activities at the herring run. When the old gristmill at Stony Brook is grinding corn for the tourists in July and August, the town regularly dams up the pond at its outlet to create a sufficient head of water to turn the great wooden overshot wheel. The combined effects of seasonal damming and variations in rainfall can cause the pond shoreline to encroach or recede as much as twenty feet in places, creating beaches of a generally swampy character.

For all these reasons, even the nearby residents of Lower Mill Pond do not use it much for bathing, preferring to drive several miles to some other, less fertile pond or ocean beach where they do not have to share the waters with so many other forms of life. Its most regular visitors are fishermen, who are lured by the native fish—white and yellow perch, pickerel, small- and largemouth bass, bluegills, pumpkinseeds, sunfish, pond suckers, bullheads, and others—that abound there, which they take in small boats in summer and through holes in the ice in winter.

Lower Mill is uncommonly full of life at all seasons of the year, but it reaches flood tide in summer. Then the shallows near the shore are thick with polliwogs basking in the lukewarm water, small black ones an inch long and the much larger, second-year bullfrog tadpoles, their rear legs already well formed and kicking. By the second week in July, hundreds of the smaller polliwogs emerge onto the stretches of low beach as tiny toadlings, now only half an inch long without their tails, that go hopping through the short, green grass and moss patches like some Lilliputian army.

Usually a banded water snake can be seen weaving casually among the purple-spiked patches of pickerelweed. Painted turtles rest on half-submerged pieces of driftwood or dive suddenly beneath floating lily pads. And all along the shore, stands of highbush blueberry, viburnum, azaleas, and other shrubs form impenetrable wet tangles within which the splashings, ploppings, gruntings, and chirpings of unseen life are constantly going on.

The pond is also unexcelled for summer nightlife on Cape Cod. On warm evenings the bullfrogs commence their *juggam!* calls in a deep, rippling crescendo that begins somewhere out on the long marsh spit at the narrows and swells around the shoreline like a wave breaking along a curving shore. To their basso continuo are shortly added the rhythms and cries of other voices: the dry, toneless screams of land toads, a myriad of insect obbligatos, the coughs and gurgles of gulls roosting far out in the center of the pond, the flat croaks of herons taking off from reedy cover to begin their night foraging, and the soft but distinctive percussive flaps of fin and tail scattered across the pond's dark, wide surface as the fish rise to their evening meal.

The pond, as I have said, enjoys no special protection or isolation. By a combination of luck and the very biological richness of its waters, it has thus far not suffered the fate of many similar ponds whose shorelines have been scraped, strangled, or smothered by excessive human presence and "improvements." It is ringed only sparsely with houses, which have kept a respectful distance back from its edges. The lush and erosion-resistant covers of its slopes have not been replaced by manicured, heavily fertilized lawns draining into its waters. These same waters are too warm for trout, so that it has also escaped the kind of "reclamation" practiced by the state in many other local ponds—a process generally consisting of chemically asphyxiating all the native or "trash" fish and replacing them with hatchery-raised trout.

And yet I realize that Lower Mill Pond remains vulnerable to future exploitation, overdevelopment, and misuse, as well as to the unpredictable influences of such things as acid rain or the long-term effects of the neaby "sanitary landfill," which may represent an unrecognized time bomb. Still, for the moment at least, its waters remain essentially undisturbed, its extraordinary plant and animal diversity flourishes in unredeemed, heathen health, its cup of life runneth rank and over. Here, on its shores, a man may still stand and put the electric human summer at a distance, the spirit may go out and claim such pools of peace for its own.

2

At the south end of Lower Mill Pond, half a mile across the water from the herring-run outlet, there is a low stretch of shoreline that has for generations been used as a fisherman's landing by residents and perennial visitors. Access to this landing is over a pair of badly eroded dirt tracks that drop off the far turn of a new road for a small subdivision and then run beneath two sets of high-voltage transmission lines. A short wooden dock pokes out into the water from the pond's edge. Here in summer I keep a rowboat, as do several others.

On a muggy morning in early July I go down to the shore of the landing and wade out into the shallow water where my boat is moored, a small, red-painted wooden punt that swings and rocks in the light westerly breeze like a tethered pony. The water is warm against my legs, so warm that it is like moving into a denser atmosphere rather than into a different medium, a change of texture more than of temperature.

The pond is not nearly as clear as it was a few weeks ago. Since then the upper layers have bloomed with microscopic algae, and a blizzard of green flakes floats suspended beneath the surface. Each flake is made up of from three to five tiny, round, single-celled plants. Though the presence of the algae clouds the water, it is from this humble and universal basis that the remarkable richness of plant and animal life in this pond springs.

Up through this light green algal snow, the bright red form of a velvet water mite paddles toward me. About the size and shape of an engorged dog tick, this brilliantly colored arachnid is an able swimmer and predator. When I lift it out of the water on my fingertip, however, it droops and melts into a shapeless tear of blood. I lower it back into the pond, where it regains its form and continues on its eight-legged way.

Swarming around the boat, just below the surface, are large, dark patches of tiny swimming creatures that look like hordes of aquatic insect larvae. They are, in fact, masses of baby ale-wives, still less than an inch long, but already schooling in wide circles like the adults, the basic herring rhythms innate in their tiny bodies.

I have already seen other herring fry, only slightly larger and older than these, being flipped down through the rushing waters of the fish ladder like cut blades of grass as they begin their precarious descent to an even more precarious saltwater world. The spring run of adult alewives is a dramatic and colorful spectacle, yet somehow these tiny fry seem to surpass their parents in sheer daring. (The fact that, from our point of view, they have no "choice" in the matter does not diminish the heroism of their undertaking.) They travel alone; no adult leads them out or shows them where to go. Only a minuscule percentage will survive to mature in the ocean and return here to spawn in three to five years. Where do they go? Some tagged fish from this area have been found in the Chesapeake Bay region to the south and as far afield as Norway. Why do they go so far? And how do they navigate their return with such precision?

"We go" is all their silent forms say, and they slip away before my approach, whirling off in miniature schools like underwater leaves blown along the shore.

Untying the mooring line of the rowboat, I hear the faint sound of a passing jet out of Boston booming high overhead. As though in response, the hidden bullfrogs along the shore commence grunting with a loud, vibrating, loosely rhythmic din. Invisible among the reeds, the frogs' pulsing chorus reminds me of the booming of ice expanding across the frozen pond in January. It is the voice of the pond itself in a summer idiom.

As I climb into the boat and launch myself out onto the water, its bright, broad surface expands away from me with wind-riffled promise. This surface is a great, changing interface of water and air, penetrated with life that is constantly dipping into, rising from, or moving over it. From the shore to the west, a pair of kingfishers swoop and rattle from bush to bush in their usual manner. The seasons do not seem to change their ways much. Big-headed, massive-billed, with a fierce flat-topped crest, the slate blue male, lacking the rusty bellyband of the female, swings out from the marsh spit up to a height of twenty feet out over the water, hangs there for ten seconds or more with great fluttering energy—the hovering motion of kestrels, peregrines, terns, all the strong stoopers and divers—then swings away again, its submerged prey unaware that it has escaped the passing of this iridescent angel of death.

Swallows are also out over the pond, emerald-backed tree swallows, with a few rough-wings sprinkled among them, banking and wheeling after flying insects. One skips along the surface, dipping its beak into the pond every few yards. Swallows even drink on the wing.

Far out in the center of the pond, a flock of gulls sated from their morning feeding at the nearby dump, form a white circle in the center of the pond, resting as light as dust motes upon it. Every now and then the entire flock lifts suddenly, in a beautiful, upward, revolving motion, circling out wider and wider over the blue waters like airborne ripples. The larger black-backed gulls (also called minister gulls) are deeper voiced and more aggressive than the herring gulls, and appear to have increased in numbers this year.

From the south a trio of black-headed laughing gulls fly out over the pond, visitors from the newly established colony on Monomoy Island, eight miles to the southeast in Nantucket Sound. Near the boat a single least tern hovers, also miles from its nesting colony on some saltwater beach. It flutters and dives, bomberlike, piercing the surface and rising again, empty billed, flinging out spray from its wings like silver rays. Alewives are not the only ocean species to use this inland pond.

Accepting all this—the rattling plunges of the saber-beaked kingfishers, the delicate dips and plucks of the swallow bills, the acrobatics of coupled darning needles, and the sudden slaps of leaping perch—is the mutable and unbroken film of the pond surface. It bisects the sunning painted and spotted turtles, the green frogs squatting like glowing jewels in the shaded shallows, the silent stalking legs of a great blue heron. It floats lily pads, duckweed, rafts of marsh grass, and supports the crossing of water striders, spiders, wind-blown pine pollen, and the red hull of my small boat across its placid expanse.

As I row westward along the edge of the shore, the deep, sweet smell of lake vegetation rises like a perfume, while brilliant mosaics of electric-blue damselflies rest like diadems on the backs of basking painted turtles. As I approach them, the damsels dart off and the turtles dive, but one of the latter scurries along the shallow bottom beside the boat. I reach in and pluck it out. It is not a painted turtle but a musk turtle, the smallest turtle in New England and one of the oddest in appearance.

The musk turtle has an egg-shaped shell about four inches long, the color of mud, covered with a considerable growth of algae and slime. This gives the creature, in the words of the herpetologist James D. Lazell, Jr., the look of "an over-size ripe olive pit, such as you often find in ashtrays after cocktail parties." It has a long, beaked snout, flattened at the tip, and this, combined with a toothless overbite, produces a rather goofy look. The animal's only distinguishing coloration is a pair of yellowish stripes on either side of the head, which part to go around each eye, one above and one below. This may serve to distract some predators such as herons, which like to stab their prey in the eye.

The musk turtle has the reputation of being the most aquatic of our freshwater turtles, spending nearly its entire life in the water and emerging only to lay its eggs in rotten stumps and clumps of vegetation near the shore. Nevertheless, I have frequently seen them sunning themselves on clumps of marsh grass or pieces of wood next to the more numerous painted turtles.

Being a pond scavenger, it spends most of its time crawling about in the bottom muck, a trait that might endear it to those who complain about the abundant aquatic vegetation in these warm-water ponds, since its constant traveling about is said to inhibit bottom plant growth. On the other hand, this action tends to keep the mud stirred up and the water murky—from which you might conclude that we are not greatly considered, one way, or the other, in its bottom perambulations.

The musk turtle's common name and its scientific label, *Sternotherus odoratus*, both derive from a set of glands near its tail. These glands produce a strong musky odor that has also earned it the nicknames of Stinkpot and Stinkin' Jenny. The smell is pungent, to be sure, but hardly deserving of its malodorous reputation. It closely resembles the smell of the pond bottom itself, which is not surprising. The scent is said to be produced by the turtle in times of stress and also to attract its mate, functions similar to those of our own sweat.

When I turn the reptile over in my hand, it squirms and claws the air. Its underside is infested with scores of small freshwater leeches that are hooked onto the exposed flesh between the shell and its small plastron, or belly plate. The musk turtle supports not only a forest of algae on its back but also a jungle of bloodsuckers on its underparts.

Prying off one of the larger leeches from a mass just above the left shoulder, I place it on the blade of one of the shipped oars. The parasite is about an inch long and shaped like a candlepin, with a sucking disc at each end. It attaches its larger rear end to the surface of the oar and raises itself up, cobralike, elongating its body to nearly twice its original length and groping about blindly in the unacccustomed air with its pin-sized head.

Then it begins to move, in inchworm fashion, attaching its head disc firmly and drawing up its rear half, reattaching the tail and then extending itself forward again. With its hooked sucking discs the leech seems able to fix itself firmly to very hard, smooth surfaces such as the turtle shell, my knifeblade, and my fingernail.

This creature's common name is, fittingly enough, the turtle leech. *Placobdella parasitica* is one of some 300 species of freshwater leeches in the United States, most of which, contrary to popular belief, are not found in steamy southern swamps but in the more numerous ponds and lakes of the glaciated northern states. The turtle leech is a semipermanent blood parasite, remaining on its host until the breeding season, when it becomes quite a graceful swimmer.

In addition to their strange anatomies and sanguineous feeding habits, leeches have developed some rather unusual mating habits. Most species are hermaphroditic, containing both male and female reproductive organs. When two turtle leeches copulate, each individual implants spermatophores—hard, club-shaped bundles of sperm—on the ventral surface of the other. Despite the presence of a genital pore through which the eggs are eventually laid, these spermatophores *bore* their way through the belly wall of the impregnated leech into the ovaries, where they fertilize the eggs.

Even more than its complex and somewhat bizarre life history, however, what strikes me most now, looking at the leech as it waves about on the blade of the oar, is its remarkable appearance. This small aquatic worm—as repulsive, blind, and mechanical as it may appear to us—is nonetheless as exquisitely fashioned and as lushly designed as the flight feathers of a snow goose or the scales of a swallowtail-butterfly wing. Its slimy back is as boldly painted as a copperhead's, adorned with beautiful butterscotch patterns on a richly brown body, with tints of red and green scattered throughout.

These patterns are produced by a highly complex coloration system beneath the leech's skin composed of three different types of pigment granules and chromatophores. The turtle leech can apparently vary the size of the chromatophores at will, and thus control the shade and intensity of its body hues. It will also turn darker as the light grows brighter, and vice versa.

What possible purpose, one might ask, is served by such bright and intricate designs, changeable at will, on a creature that spends most of its life on the underside of a reptile that spends most of *its* life in lightless muck? And the answer one gets is—none. Apparently, with all this highly refined pigmenting equipment, the turtle leech shows no sign of color adaptation whatsoever.

In such cases, it would seem, nature is purposelessly extravagant, tempting me to believe in a force that creates for its own pleasure merely. But bright coloration is characteristic of leeches as a group, and it is likely that such seemingly superfluous decoration will eventually be found to perform some function in their life cycle.

Functional or not, however, the leech's tapestried hide is revelation that all existence is, for whatever reason, ineffably *finished*, extravagantly executed down to the last intricate, beautiful, even possibly useless detail. This minor reptilian parasite mutely proclaims that nature has an unquenchable passion for fine work, even in her most bizarre creatures. She forms the hooked maw of a bloodsucker with the same precision and balance of design as the talon of a hawk or the petal on a beach-plum blossom. Like Ferrara's last duchess, her smiles go everywhere. Emerson, over a hundred years ago, might have had the mud turtle and its leeches in mind when he wrote,

> But in the mud and scum of things,
> There alway, alway something sings.

At the narrows, where Upper Mill Pond flows into Lower Mill, a marsh spit has built out several hundred feet into the water, a long, jutting, grassy finger created by silt depositions from the upper pond. Among its deltalike maze of rivulets, reeds, shrubs, and hummocks can be found, at various times of the year, nesting Canada geese, black ducks, redwings and green herons, migrating pied grebes and snowy egrets, wintering great blue herons, and an occasional rail. For the past few years a lone osprey has stopped here in autumn, hovering on bent wings high above the narrows, waiting for a fish.

As I maneuver toward the end of this spit, a pair of geese fly in from the east. Angling down toward the water, they throw back their broadly cupped wings to break speed, thrust out webbed feet in unison like landing gear, and then, cackling all the while and jockeying headlong down through the air, descend together in a splashy, but perfectly controlled, landing. In the next moment all that wildly moving equipment of feather, bone, and muscle is stilled and folded up, like a pair of eyelids, into two composed long-necked forms that paddle swiftly around the end of the spit away from me and are gone.

These are the pond's resident pair of Canada geese. It is doubtful that they are true wild migratory geese, since most evidence suggests that this species historically nested only sporadically in Massachusetts. Most of the Cape's present breeding geese are the descendants of flocks of hundreds, sometimes thousands, of captives kept by wealthy sportsmen in the early part of this century as live decoys and call birds. These birds were released after live decoying was outlawed, in 1935, and now their descendants are common as year-round residents on many of our reedier ponds. These semidomestic ferals are frequently fed by shorefront owners, who are at first delighted by their presence and then curse the geese when they begin to overpopulate a pond and foul its beaches and water with their excessive droppings.

These two, however, if not truly wild, are at least solitary and wary, arriving each March with the first southerly winds and rarely letting me get within thirty yards of them. For the past several years they have raised a brood of young on the pond, nesting either out on the spit or in the dense shrubbery bordering the shore behind it.

I row out around the tip of the spit, where the sluggish, dissipated stream from Upper Mill Pond slides slowly out and mixes with the waters of Lower Mill. There, along the shore of a small cove on its far side, the two Canadas paddle among the emerging yellow globes of the pond lilies. Between them is a gray, fuzzy adolescent, about two-thirds grown, swimming earnestly along with its parents as they glide on with a slight rocking motion. Several weeks earlier I watched five small, downy goslings following these adults about the pond; now only one remains. Snappers.

The geese begin to browse in the pickerelweed, noisily crunching its long sagitate leaves in their serrated bills. After several minutes of feeding they swim silently off again. How peacefully they glide along, as serene as the swan boats in Boston's Public Gardens. What silent violence cries out from their reduced numbers!

As I row strongly and smoothly through the morning stillness and growing warmth, through the rafts of already-yellowing lily pads, smelling the clean fecundity of a pond flowing in concert with itself and all its connected waters, straining back and looking up into the high, sealed summer sky spread with floury clouds, I feel rich and lucky, possessor of more than I could ever have asked for or deserved. Each unmeasured moment is the extension of a lease I never held, a gift whose very breadth and extent removes any possible anxiety over losing it.

Then I see something else, another bit of pond life, whose unexpected appearance itself reminds me of the reduced expectations by which we unconsciously live today. Foraging in the tall grass at the head of the narrows is a young black-crowned night heron, a brownish bird with a yellow eye, heavily streaked breast, speckled back, and thick, pale yellow legs. Beyond this immature heron, perched in the dead, zigzag limbs of a flooded stand of tupelos, is a quartet of adult birds. The four mature herons are strange, nocturnal-looking creatures, of a colorless, moonlit hue even at midday, hunching in the background like extras on the set of a horror movie. Sitting so intensely motionless, with their restrained lowered head plumes and distinctly outlined, black-and-white body plumage, they look more like cardboard cutouts, cartoon birds, than real herons. But as I pull nearer, the adults suddenly launch themselves with a leap, defecating in unison as they rise, heads snaked back, chicken-yellow legs rocking in time with their broad, flat wingbeats as they slowly retract their feet and utter the distinct, guttural call that gives them their colloquial name: *Quawk!*

But it is the young night heron that holds my attention. Perhaps still unfledged, or preoccupied with a frog or fish it has spotted, it remains among the reeds. Body flattened to the water, head thrust somewhat forward but still partially drawn, it stands motionless for nearly ten minutes before it finally strikes and misses.

I watch this immature bird with keen interest, for it is the first sign in years that these herons are breeding in the area.

Black-crowned night herons were formerly abundant on the Cape, nesting in large colonies of a few hundred pairs up and down the peninsula and in a few enormous rookeries of several thousand birds in the Barnstable area. Today, though adults frequently roost in these dead tupelos during the summer, there are only a few, scattered breeding colonies along the Cape's entire length.

Stony Brook Valley itself was once the home of a sizable colony of black-crowned night herons, estimated at 200 to 300 pairs. On September 18, 1952, the entire colony was shotgunned out by state game officers after a nearby resident complained about the noise and offensive odors produced by the birds. Some local protests of the shooting were made to the Massachusetts Audubon Society, but the officers apparently had the proper state and federal permits. When the local paper made inquiries, the state game warden "gave a strongly worded declaration that it was none of this newspaper's business."

Today, black-crowned night herons are no longer listed as a regular nesting species on Cape Cod. Overhunted by the millinary trade in the early part of the century, exterminated by "public-health measures" such as the massacre at Stony Brook, and poisoned by the bath of pesticides spread on the marshes in the 1950s and 1960s, the herons' original numbers have been drastically reduced. Furthermore, quawks are very sensitive to human presence, and the combined filling of wetlands and rapid development of suitable habitat over the last several decades have left only a few, isolated places where the remaining herons can breed. Today it is estimated that no more than a few dozen birds return to our local wetlands each summer. If the estimate is accurate, then the four adults and one juvenile on the pond this morning represent a sizable proportion of the Cape's entire quawk population.

It is possible that the large heronries of the past constituted a genuine public nuisance to those living nearby, or even presented water-quality problems as a result of their abundant excrement. But they also represented an irreplaceable dimension, an alternative reality to the Cape's increasingly human face, which we apparently could not endure in the past and can no longer support.

It is noon. The wind has died, the air has grown hazy, and the surface of the water is opaque and opalescent, like a silken cloth spread in the sun. I have taken refuge from the increasing heat in the shade of some beech limbs that overhang another cove on the northwest shore. Resting in the boat, which is tied to one of the muscular, cantilevered trunks, I find myself thinking seriously about taking a dip in the pond to cool off. Then, just as I am about to slip over the side, a patch of water some sixty feet offshore begins to roil furiously. The circle of disturbance is roughly twenty feet across and looks and sounds like that made by schools of bluefish feeding violently out in the calm Bay, though nothing shows but the splashing water. The noisy thrashing continues unabated for several minutes, then ceases as suddenly as it began. I untie the boat and row over to investigate, but find nothing—no fish, no insects, not even scales or leaves—only a few patches of bubbles.

Could it be herring spawning? But it is late for them, and they tend to lay their eggs in shallower water. Eels perhaps? Bottom gas? A vacationing Loch Ness monster that has migrated up Stony Brook? I can almost believe that the pond itself is alive and given to fits of temper. Whatever it is, this small mystery has momentarily chilled my desire for a swim.

But as mysteries often do, this one soon insists on revealing itself. Continuing along the shore, I quickly encounter more splashing and draw near a mass of large, swarming fish, darting and thrashing about as though engaged in some turbulent underwater ballet. They are larger than alewives, nearly a foot and a half in length, dark green and thick bodied, with round, whalelike heads. They lack the adipose fin of bass, and their pelvic fins are placed far back on their bodies. They are pond suckers.

What confused me at first was the energy and flamboyance of their performance, so unlike the normal behavior of these sluggish, bottom-dwelling fish. The pond sucker, a member of the carp family, is not highly regarded by most people, when it is regarded at all. Although one of the larger and more wide-spread freshwater fish, it is rarely seen. Slow-moving and dark-colored, it spends most of its time among the vegetation and mud of pond and stream bottoms, scavenging with its thick, fleshy lips, which are placed on the underside of its head.

Suckers have been called the vacuum cleaners of the fish world, moving along and sucking up small snails, vegetable debris, worms, insect larvae, and fish eggs. Anglers disdain them, for although their flesh is said to be quite sweet and tasty when cooked fresh, it is very bony. When hooked, suckers do not put up much of a fight, and so lack "game value" as well.

Locally, they have a reputation for consuming enormous quantities of herring eggs. I have myself seen them lounging near spawning alewives, then moving in lazily to scoop up some of the eggs as soon as they are laid. But the herring eggs appear to be more of a seasonal delicacy than a staple for the sucker. At any rate, the two species have lived in productive balance with one another for centuries, and such predation represents for the herring just one more station in the predator-studded gauntlet they must run each year.

Even among those naturalists who grant them a rightful place in our waters, suckers seem to elicit at best a somewhat lethargic enthusiasm. Thoreau, who once made friends with a trout, described them as "dull and blundering fellows, fond of the mud," and John Hay, a writer hardly ever given to abusive epithets, writes them off as "a crude, crass, lazy taster of a fish."

So most of the time the poor pond sucker meanders along

our pond bottoms, slow and gluttonous, dragging a somewhat disparaging reputation behind it. Yet now I see that even this fish is capable of rising to the quickness of life. The males in the water are performing their mating "dance," rising up to the surface in a noisy flurry. This is apparently a late spurt of breeding activity, which usually takes place in late May. More than fifty fish are in the group. The males, somewhat darker than the females, have distinct, reddish stripes along their sides, which may serve to trigger breeding behavior in their mates.

As one of the somewhat larger and lighter-colored females sidles in among some protruding rocks, she is quickly joined by several males who begin to caress and rub their bodies up against her. Sometimes eight or nine males gather around a single female, and then all at once there is a burst of thrashing and flipping, lasting only a second or two, as the males release their milt into the water. Following this, the group disperses instantly, as though alarmed, regrouping again in half a minute or so.

Often several of these grouping and dispersing motions take place at once. A single female swims between two rocks, followed by two males that wedge in on either side of her. Suddenly they begin to flurry, vibrating rapidly in place for several seconds, causing the water to foam up around them. During the spawning act itself, the lateral stripes of the males turn a deep, brilliant scarlet, glowing among the dark green backs and the light-shattered water on the surface.

Accompanying the oblivious suckers are several other, smaller fish—perch and pumpkinseeds mostly—swimming calmly among them. These appear to be following the spawning suckers, eating up their eggs as they are laid, much as the suckers at other times eat theirs. Eggs in the fish world end up as food more often than as progeny, and those of the suckers seem to be no exception. Their fry are also favored food for such game species as trout and pike, which may actually flourish better when suckers are present.

Here for once, then, these suckers, so often portrayed as sotted gleaners, are themselves caught up in a rhythmic, colorful frenzy of procreation, fulfilling at once more needs and uses than either they or I may realize. So totally caught up in their passion are they that when I lean out of the boat directly over them, they show no response. Only when I stretch my hand down and touch for an instant their surfacing, glistening backs do they scare and scatter down into deep, invisible waters.

I did not intend to stay out all day on the pond, but as the afternoon wears on and a refreshing breeze springs up out of the northeast, I find it harder and harder to think of good reasons for turning back. Grasping the oars again, I continue to explore the northern shore, passing a high, pine-studded knoll. At the base of the knoll is Seagull Rock, a large glacial boulder lying half in the water, so called because it is a favorite lookout perch for gulls, whose droppings have given it a white-washed appearance easily distinguishable from the opposite shore. From the rock, I pass out across the opening of the funnel-shaped channel that winds and narrows down to the head of the herring run.

I am now exactly halfway around the pond from my starting point. The wind appears to be blowing directly back toward the dock, and so, shipping my oars, I move to the stern seat, lean against the backrest, and settle down to let the breeze blow the little boat gently back across the pond. Seated in the stern, I become a kind of weighted pivot, so that the bow of the boat rises up and becomes a perfect weather vane, shirting with the slightest shift in the wind to give me an instant report of any change in our heading.

Such moments as this on the pond are among its best. As I float across its surface, like a red mote across a giant blue eye, the changing breezes seem to revolve the entire body of water before me in a smoothly turning panorama. I pass close by the circle of gulls in its center, the white pupil of its blue iris. Now they are actively bathing, splashing, and tossing themselves on the surface. Every so often one turns all the way over on its back, kicking its legs high in the air and thrashing about like a horse in a dust pit. Yet as I drift by, I notice that the flock as a whole remains facing the wind and seems to stay in roughly the same location, relative to the shore. When not bathing, it seems, the gulls are all constantly paddling gently, unnoticeably together beneath the surface to maintain their position in the center of the pond. Like all animals, they must continually readjust their stance toward the world, if only to stay in place.

There is only one other boat out on the pond today. Over against the eastern shore, where the wooded banks fall down steeply and several large rocks jut out of the water, I see Bill Lazarus's small outboard. It is painted sky blue, the blue of the old Cape wagons, and Bill is sitting in its stern, trolling among the rocks as he has for over forty years.

I have been out fishing with Bill Lazarus several times. He taught me how to net minnows along the shallow beach and to find the bass holes. He knows this pond through long, affectionate intimacy, and the decades of summers spent out on its shining waters have left their mark on his softly folded, blotched, and sun-freckled face. He remembers when its hills were as bare as the Yorkshire moors and his was the only house along its shores. He has aged with it, and his once-rich voice now vacillates between deep tones and soft, breathy squeaks. But his eyes are dark brown, kind, and clear. (Our eyes, like the feathers of birds, are the only things about us that seem to remain perpetually young.) Now, in the fullness of age, he has gathered his life about this pond, including his son's family, which lives on the opposite bluff across the narrows.

Now eighty-nine and a retired New York banker, Bill Lazarus grew up in the notorious Hell's Kitchen section of the Lower West Side. As a young boy he sold newspapers at Sixth Avenue and Thirty-fourth Street, "a corner I had to defend with my life." He describes himself as "a three-time high-school dropout," but he managed to take some language courses at City College of New York, which he says was more of a high school than a college then. Once he was arrested and spent a night in jail for shooting craps in front of the Algonquin Hotel. His mother refused to bail him out; his uncle thought it would be good for him; but his Spanish teacher came to see him in his cell and told him, "Now William, this doesn't mean a thing. You're doing well in your lessons—be back in class Monday morning."

In 1908, at the age of sixteen, he sought "economic advancement" by shipping out on steerage to Havana. ("Why Havana?" I asked him. "It was the closest place to New York they spoke Spanish then," he explained.) The day he arrived, he applied to the port bank for a job, was asked whether he could add and subtract, and on the basis of those talents was offered a position as teller for twenty-five dollars a month—the beginning of a sixty-three-year career in international finance.

During his long career he traveled all over the world, wintering in Havana until 1959 and subsequently in Florida. But each spring since 1937 he and his wife, Freda, have returned to the shores of Lower Mill Pond, to their small house tucked in among the pines on its eastern bluff, and to the waters that Bill loves to fish.

Fishing is his excuse for being on the pond, as "observation" is mine. He sometimes likes to put me in the position of an "authority"; but though we have come to know the pond in our own ways, they often overlap. Now, as we pass one another at a distance of some sixty yards, he waves in greeting, points at the gulls on the water between us, and hails me in that half-resonant voice: "Say, what do you call those black-backed gulls."

"Right!" I shout back, laughing, and for a moment he is the old Adam, naming the birds.

Thoreau once said if you sit quietly in one spot in the woods, all of the life in the forest will soon appear before you. Here, sitting in a boat on the pond, letting the wind move me about like a leaf, I am almost inundated by its various lives. As I float across its murky depths, the fecundity of its water bubbles up beneath me. Swarms of apostrophic, transparent herring fry gestate in its warm shallows. Herds of fat, bloated polliwogs bask in the sun, leisurely sprouting legs. Turtles, frogs, and muskrats drop from its banks, plopping like ripe fruit. Perch and pickerel rise from the bottom, pricking small ripples that dilate in waters turned golden by the declining sun, while herons, gulls, ducks, and geese spring up from its resilient surface like autumn seeds in the wind.

From one side of the pond comes the raw screech of a crane loading scrap metal at the dump, while from the other side, in a house hidden on the hillside, Bill Lazarus's baby granddaughter begins to squall inconsolably. Somehow these human noises possess a quality primitive or elemental enough to blend in with the more natural sounds of the pond. Or perhaps its viscous, flowing surface is flexible enough to mix even our cacophony into its subtle and complex harmony. Even the kingfisher seems subdued now as he swings out over the approaching dock, his harsh clattering softened, elasticized by the coming of dusk.

CHAPTER *10*

Scratching

1
_____

North of the Mill Ponds, at the lower end of Stony Brook
Valley, where the low glacial hills spread apart and slope down
toward sea level, the herring river flows through a large tidal
gate beneath the state highway, and in so doing changes both
its name and its character. From Stony Brook, a shallow, swift-
flowing, freshwater stream, it becomes Paine's Creek, a deeper,
wider, saltwater tidal river that elbows its way another half a
mile north through broad stretches of salt marsh, finally emp-
tying through a break in the shoreline out onto the wide tidal
flats of Cape Cod Bay.

One day in early spring, while raking for sea clams at low
tide, nearly a mile offshore from the mouth of Paine's Creek, I
hit what I first thought was an enormous clam. When I finally
managed to work it out of the sand, however, it turned out to
be the skull of a blackfish, or pilot whale, a relatively small
cetacean that was once commonly hunted in the waters of the

Bay. It was a large head, about thirty inches long and nearly two feet wide. Lying there on the dark sands, with its long, sloping upper jaw, it reminded me of one of those hollow-eyed cow skulls that bleakly dot the western deserts. But no desert skull harbors such a diverse community of life as this one did. The whale head was dark and discolored with marine algae. Ribbons of *Fucus*, or rockweed, streamed out of its nostrils. A green crab crawled agilely out of one of the eye sockets to see what had disturbed its home, and the soft, porous, crumbling gray bone was decorated with the mottled, pearly pink hulls of attached slipper shells. There was a flowering of life, if not thought, in this ancient head; it seemed to stare up at me out of the muddy sand with its dark, hollow eyes and speak mutely of another age. As I left it and walked back toward shore with my bucket of clams, I passed lines and broken arcs of post stumps, hairy with fine, dark green seaweed. These were the sheared-off remnants of the many fishing weirs that used to trace their elaborate patterns of poles and nets across these flats. Both were reminders of a time, not too far distant, when black-fish were still a common sight in these waters and men harvested an earnest living, and not merely an occasional bucket of clams, from these shores.

How well-used these long, low flats have been! And how remarkably unscathed they have remained, even today, despite the increasing intensity of human activity. Everywhere over their dark, wet plains are spread the artifacts of past human use: the skeletons of whales, the stumps of fish weirs, crumbling stone breakwaters at the old packet landing, occasional broken bottles of bootlegged whiskey, tossed overboard at night during Prohibition by local rumrunners, the blackened hulks of small wrecks and derelict vessels, alternately buried and exhumed by shifting currents and bars. There even appears, on rare occasions, a human skull.

This, as Thoreau might have put it, is the only genuine Historical Society of Cape Cod, its exhibits artfully arranged in spacious, authentic settings, frequently changed, open to view twice a day, seven days a week, at no charge, their lessons clear and needing no human labels.

2

These expansive tidal flats are peculiar to the Bay side of the Cape. On the south side, or Nantucket Sound shore, meager tides of only three or four feet reveal barely a hundred feet of sea bottom at dead low. In Cape Cod Bay, by contrast, the tides heave and collapse ten feet or more on new moons, sweeping out over the sands for well over a mile in places. I have heard it claimed that Brewster has the largest area of tidal flats of any town on the eastern seaboard.

Every twelve and a half hours the ebbing tide reveals a vast drowned world of extremes, contrasts, specialized needs, appalling barrenness, and, at times, equally appalling abundance. Despite such obvious differences as its marine life forms, the inner flats are in fact a kind of biological wet desert: visually barren, alkaline, lacking in fresh water, and subject to sudden extremes of temperature and moisture. As with the animals of a dry desert during the day, the permanent inhabitants of the flats remain largely underground and out of sight at low tide, emerging only with the twice-daily flood, the aquatic night, to feed and be fed upon. When a dry wind skips over the exposed flats, it can kick up a sandstorm that will sting the face and blind the eyes. And when a stranded fish or bird or marine mammal dies here, the legions of gulls, which have been sitting patiently on the bars amid the exposed whitened shells of sea clams, descend to the feast with the same horrible enthusiasm and grim grace as vultures do.

But it is not just their dramatic display of tidal movement or the harsh extremes to which the life that lives there must adapt that makes the flats a special environment. They also offer us challenges and connections in a wider world. In contrast to the maze of woods around my house, the flats pose a problem of orientation rather than one of entry. Out there one finds few or no landmarks to go by; distance and size become notoriously deceptive, and men have been lost and drowned on the far bars when sudden fogs come in with the tide. Still, these wet plains are of superlative extent and present opportunities for exposure and encounter that are unparalleled in sheer magnitude anywhere else on the Cape's, if not the continent's, shores.

Like most local residents, however, I usually go out on the flats not for adventure but for the pragmatic and rather tame purpose of gathering clams. "Clamming" is a generic term used to refer to the harvesting of a broad spectrum of shellfish, including oysters, soft-shell or steamer clams, mussels, sea clams, razor clams, and even scallops. All of these shellfish can be found to a greater or lesser degree in various parts of the Bay, but in Brewster, owing to local conditions, "clamming" is generally understood to refer to the pedestrian pursuit of a single mollusk—*Venus mercenaria*, the quahog or hard-shell clam.

Some of these conditions are environmental. The lack of proper salinity and substrate, for instance, makes our local flats unsuitable for oysters. But it is more the innate qualities of the quahog that have combined to make it the true shellfish of Brewster's waters. Widely distributed, the quahog tends to occupy a middle ground, neither so far in as the steamer clam (which, easily reached, has been virtually dug out here for years) nor so far out as the sea clam (which can be raked only on the lowest moon tides). It can thus be gathered on most ordinary tides and, in contrast to the swift-burrowing razor clam, requires only moderate skill and effort to catch. Also, unlike the mercurial scallop, the quahog varies little in abundance from year to year.

Plentiful and dependable, these mollusks are also "sociable," in that they lend themselves not only to human enterprise but to encouragement as well. Local quahogs are not, strictly speaking, a wild crop. For years the town has run a seeding program to replenish the supply, enforced quotas, and rotated the sections of flats open to digging on a seasonal basis. In this sense they can be considered "managed," though the quahogs' ultimate success and maintenance still depend far more on the overall health and influence of the Bay than on human manipulation.

Perhaps it is making a virtue of necessity, but the quahog seems not only the most available but also the most rewarding of local shellfish to harvest. Any form of clamming is always much more than the mere taking and eating of a bivalve mollusk, and the quahog's positive qualities go far beyond its reliability and accessibility. When dug up, quahogs have a rich, weathered, blue-and-gray cast to them, as though they had lain beneath the mud for ages, forming slowly like minerals in the earth. Their smooth, rounded, gracefully asymmetrical shape fits satisfyingly in the palm, and their shells are covered with patterns of growth rings that reflect their environment: rippled sand flats, expanding waves, a concentrically spreading world. They take their color and form from where they live and possess that perfection of completeness, of circumference, like the compassed tufts of beach grass whose blade tips draw rings around themselves in the dune sand.

Moreover, we always seem to become part of whatever we pursue. The soft-shell or steamer clam, for instance, is a serious, single-minded creature, deeply entrenched in its hole and industriously siphoning its food through a long, extended "foot." To catch one, the clam digger must squat down or bend far over, keeping his gaze directedly downward to the clam, following it with his thoughts into its dark, mucky hole, and prying it out, not only with his short-handled rake and fingers, but also with the intensity of his concentration. Thus the digging of steamers tends to be a self-absorbed, introspective activity, and when engaged in it I find that I catch a sense of my surroundings only at scattered moments, holding communion for the most part with the clam alone. Whosoever digs that clam loses a portion of the day. He grows a kind of shell over himself that blocks out sunlight.

Quahogging, on the other hand, tends to be a cleaner and more expansive business. Because the quahog is a shallow burrower, the scratcher can remain upright, coaxing rather than wrestling his quarry out of the mud with his long-handled rake. Though his concentration may be in the rake, his consciousness can remain afloat, above the mud, above the water, and he is free to cast his gaze around him and rise to the lures of the day.

3

The true Cape Codder, the local saying goes, spends more time in the water between October and May than from June to September. By this standard, at least, I may claim the status of a genuine resident, for it is during these colder months that the best quahog flats in our town are open to scratching.

Late on an afternoon in early October, when the first set of high-course tides for the month has arrived, I drive down to the Bay shore. It is less than an hour until the end of the tide's long, silent withdrawal, and the flats lie exposed, a glistening expanse of dual nature, half land and half water. I pull on my chest-high waders, hitch my rake and bucket in hand, and, with the sloping sun over my left shoulder, set out after the receding tide.

My footsteps push broad sheens of silver wetness out of the saturated sands as I go. Braided veins of water, draining out from under the slope of the beach like reversed river deltas, weave together and follow me in small, meandering streams. The flats here are strewn with the thin, brittle, empty shells of last year's scallop crop, blown ashore and frozen by winter storms; I crunch them underfoot as I go. Small groups of gulls sit quietly on the higher bars, giving me wary, sidelong glances as I pass. They are content, as always, to wait.

Soon I reach the edge of the withdrawing tide, a few hundred yards from shore. I continue out, sloshing through the shallows, and as the deepening water gradually slows my progress, the abundance of life about my feet increases. Schools of hundreds of minnows nibble at the very hem of the tide, then scatter away in shimmers like wind over water at my approach. Hermit crabs scuttle and paw across the sands in their rocking periwinkle or moon-snail shells. An occasional *Nereis*, or common seaworm, flashes by like an electric-green ribbon, and everywhere the transparent sand shrimp dart invisibly about, making tiny explosions of sand grains along the bottom.

Farther out I begin to enter the extensive beds of eelgrass, streaming northeastward in the outrunning current. If the inner flats are desertlike, these eelgrass beds are more like plains, or prairies, open eelgrasslands pocked with saltwater holes, where at the lowest tides wide, shallow rivers wind Platte-like through their shifting channels, and tiny burrows of crabs, clams, and plumed worms dot the mud and sand like miniature prairie-dog towns. Now, in the shallow water, early flocks of brant—small, darker versions of Canada geese—graze on the floating tresses of the eelgrass, and two miles out the distant roaring of the surf sounds like unseen herds of bison or antelope.

The eelgrass marks the beginning of the quahog beds. Areas of abundance shift slightly from year to year, but a few rock-weed-skirted boulders on the inner flats afford me a rough triangulation to locate myself where past experience has shown the digging to be best. Now about a quarter of a mile out and knee-deep in water, I set down my wire basket, attached by a short rope to a small Styrofoam float, and begin scratching.

"Scratching," like "clamming," can be used in a loose way to denote the gathering of any shellfish with a pronged instrument. Used properly, however, it is part of a very precise terminology and refers only to the harvesting of quahogs (and perhaps sea clams) with a quahog rake. As such, scratching is a highly accurate and descriptive term. Soft-shell and razor clams, which often lie a foot or more below the surface, must be "dug" with a clam rake, a short-handled tool with thick, bent prongs. Scallops, lying on the surface (when they are not swimming around), are more properly "raked" with an instrument very much like a garden rake with a basket attached. But quahogs generally lie just below the surface of the flats and are therefore "scratched" out.

In summer, on the more distant bars, the larger "chowder" quahogs are sometimes found with their "shoulders," or valve hinges, showing white and dry an inch or so above the mud surface. But now, in autumn, when the water in the Bay begins to turn colder, the quahogs dig in deeper, though never more than five or six inches, the depth of the rake tines. In clear, calm water, on a clean bottom, it is relatively easy to tell when you have struck one. Often, though, the water is so choppy and murky that you can hardly distinguish grassy from bare areas. Then you have to be careful not to step inadvertently into one of the "ice holes"—shallow, bare depressions in the eelgrass beds gouged out by the movement of winter ice— which can result in a sudden, chilly bath.

Under these circumstances, and especially when there is an abundance of empty scallop shells partially buried in the sand, it can be quite difficult to tell when a quahog has been struck. This is particularly true of the smaller quahogs, "cherry-stones" and "littlenecks," which give less resistance than the large chowders and often feel like small stones or clumps of empty shells. Then you must *feel* them out, using the rake handle and tines as sensory extensions of your arms, as a woodcock feels out earthworms deep in moist gound with his long, prehensile bill, or as an experienced fisherman can distinguish flounder from a skate on his line before pulling it up.

I have become convinced that a well-made quahog rake is one of those perfect tools, superbly fitted to both use and user.

A properly made rake stands slightly over four and a half feet tall and has an ash handle tapering slightly in from the end, then thickening again where it enters the socket. The six steel tines are curved and flattened to slip strongly, yet smoothly, through the mud and sand, deep enough to reach the maximum depth to which a quahog will burrow yet spaced widely enough that anything smaller than a legal-size littleneck (two-inch minimum) will fall through.

Not only is a quahog rake perfectly designed for its primary function, but it is also admirably suited for a variety of other manual tasks, such as raking salt hay off the beach for garden mulch, digging potatoes out of their hills, and plucking apples for cider out of roadside trees. It is, moreover, the most effective tool I know for clearing the formidable catbrier thickets on my lot. Its long handle allows me to keep out of harm's way, while its wide, curved tines will hook the thorny vines and pull them out, yard after barbed yard, yet afterward disengage rather easily from the mounded tangle. No other tool I know of is so at home, and of such use at all seasons on land, sea, and in between.

Scratching is in itself a highly satisfying activity. Although it superficially resembles hoeing or cultivating, it is slower, more careful work, something like pulling loose teeth from soft, rotten gums. I love to set myself against an outrunning tide, eelgrass streaming before me, and methodically rake my rows across the sandy bottom. The curved, rusted tines give a soft shush with each sweep through the sand, as I wait for the feel and sound of the hard, rocky scratch that signals a buried quahog. The lines made by the rake remind me of the pronged chalk holders used by my grade-school music teachers to draw wavy staves across the blackboard. My own moving lines strike and reveal the buried quahogs, which sing their sharp squeaks against the metal tines.

Though I usually do not need to go out more than half a

mile for quahogs, on very low tides I occasionally go out into the deep channel that runs parallel to the shoreline nearly a mile out, separating the inner flats from the farthest bars where the sea clams are found. Because this channel is only rarely shallow enough to scratch on foot, I often find untouched "honey holes" of cherrystones and littlenecks here, and fill an entire bucket with on-the-half-shell delights in fifteen minutes. There is also something euphoric about raking in such deep channels, standing chest-deep in waders in the cold, clutching water, rocked softly by the gentle swells as the current runs between the bars. As I begin, the long eelgrass streams steadily to the east, then gradually loses tension, weaves indecisively at slack water, swirling about my legs and obscuring the bottom, then slowly unfurls and streams southwesterly as the tide begins to flood.

4

There is so much life other than quahogs in these waters that on some days my rake has trouble attending to business. Its steel tines impale moon snails, green crabs, calico crabs, spider crabs, horseshoe crabs, channeled whelks, and occasionally small winter flounders buried in the mud. Once, in mid-January, I unearthed a burrowed-in sand eel—a thin, silvery fish about five inches long—which flashed and wriggled as though protesting my impertinence. It was a vibration, a bit of tangible panic in the clear, green water that darted and disappeared in an instant into the mud from which I had mis-taken it.

Above the water, I am surrounded in all seasons by birds. The bird life on the flats is not only plentiful but also rather neatly stratified from shore to deep water. In September and October the most common species along the beach are tree swallows in migration. By the hundreds they swoop low over the marsh grass that fringes the shore. Swallows do not fly in the tight formations of most shorebird flocks, but move in loose and shifting cohesions, like raiding parties. At high tide they thread among the tops of the tawny spartina stalks undulating in the waves. Frequently they pause and hover for several seconds like hummingbirds, picking off marsh insects that have climbed the grass stems to escape the tide, only to find a sharper death waiting in the swallows' beaks. As they dip and dart, the flock moves in a gradual and staggered, but steady, progression down the beach, like chips of wood carried in a longshore current, traveling slowly on, feeding as they go, toward the declining sun.

By the time these quahog beds open, in October, the peak of the "fall" shorebird migration (which actually begins in early July) has long passed, but over the inner flats at low tide there are still numbers of small sandpipers or "peep," black-bellied plovers, an occasional golden plover, scattered yellowlegs, and small flocks of ruddy turnstones (one of the happier as well as more descriptive of common bird names). Running along the sand, feeding in the shallows and tide pools, these birds stitch together all the varied terrain with their linear footprints and probing bills.

With them, as in all seasons, are the scavenger crows and gulls. Out here on the flats the ubiquitous herring and black-backed gulls give the same general impression of satisfied indolence that they do at the dump or on the pond. Standing about in flocks of varying size, they talk in low, muffled tones and hoarse cackles, like old women—seductive, self-concerned, noncommittal. But these gulls are actually more industrious than they are usually given credit for being. Often, as I go out, I see them standing in the little outrunning tidal streams, paddling backward in the mud like ducks, stirring up small crustaceans and worms, which they quickly snatch up. Better known is their habit of dropping quahogs and other shellfish on rocks, hard mud, parking lots, and even nearby golf-course cart ways to crack them open. Once, while scratching, I became aware of a large flock of gulls swarming and dipping down into the water all around me. They were skillfully plucking long, fringed, *Nereis* seaworms (which emerge from their burrows when the tide begins to flood) from just below the surface. It was a feat at which they were obviously well practiced, though they seemed just as cantankerous and bickering as ever, just as willing to harass and steal from one another as when in the midst of garbage-dump plenty.

From early May to mid-September I see the white sculptured forms of terns fishing for sand eels in short, explosive dives over the shallow Bay waters. By October, however, all but a few of these small seabirds have gathered and left for their wintering quarters in the Caribbean and South America. But an even more dramatic diving display sometimes occurs in late fall when sustained southeasterly winds blow hundreds of migrating gannets into the Bay.

One morning in mid-November, following just such a blow, I spent several hours on the outer bars sea-clamming. About seven o'clock I noticed gannets sailing close in, just beyond the bars: large, white, powerful birds that glided silently on arched, black-tipped wings nearly six feet across. There were forty or fifty in all. Most were white adults, but there were several brown speckled immatures and a few just entering adult plumage that still had some remaining speckles on their wings. They gathered gradually, out of nowhere, like a storm forming over the sea. Circling over an area half a mile north of where I was raking, they shortly began plunging after an invisible school of fish.

Gannets do not drop directly into the water as terns do, but dive diagonally downward from heights of fifty to a hundred feet, keeping their great wings outstretched until the last few feet, when they clap them swiftly shut and disappear in high bursts of white spray. Actually, the splashes were smaller than I might have expected at that height from a bird nearly as large as a swan, but gannets are extremely sleek and tapered in shape.

In contrast to a tern flock's dense, combinelike reaping of the waters, theirs was a more circular, freewheeling, dog-fight affair. For half an hour or more I watched their unexcelled display of aerial predation. Finally they flew off or, rather, dispersed, as quietly, separately, and imperceptibly as they had gathered, like a storm that gradually diminishes.

It is also during the fall scratching season that the Cape's winter waterfowl begin to appear in the Bay: arriving flocks of brant and geese, long, dark lines of migrating scoters, and the wintering sea ducks—eiders, mergansers, whistlers, old-squaw, canvasbacks, scaup, the diminutive ruddies and buffleheads— a long and varied parade that is normally not completed until mid-December.

At high tide many of these waterfowl can be seen close inshore, feeding on the eelgrass and tidal organisms. But at low tide, when I am out on the flats, I can commonly see, far out on the horizon to the north, long waves and skeins of brant and sco-ters wending over the dark waters in massive flocks of a thou-sand or more, accompanied by a distant cackling din that sounds like a chorus of wood frogs. Nearer in, a line of heavy-bodied eiders, pied drakes and drab females, fly suddenly out of the west and close overhead with rose-tinted breasts, soundless but for the rush of heavy wings. In the middle distance, patches and squadrons of tiny, bobbing buffleheads and sleek mergan-sers weave, circle, swim, and swing back and forth in endless restlessness across the choppy, blue water. Such casual, dis-tant water ballets suggest an even greater, unseen abundance. How much more uncounted bird life lies within the Bay's cir-cling arm beyond my radius of vision? Yet what I can see fills me with a waterfelt buoyancy that often leaves me standing idle, my rake and bucket forgotten, while patterns of weather wheel overhead.

Finally, though, it is the weather itself that proves to be the most powerful, suggestive, and distracting force out on the flats.

In late fall and early winter, the best low tides of the month come just at or after sundown, when the new or full moon is rising. While clamming then, I am frequently taken unawares by remarkable sunset displays. Patches of tinted light, swimming in the nearer channels, catch my eye: gradually they spread over the wet, sand-rippled plains, flowing farther out and taking me with them, becoming broad swaths and rafts of glowing colors that congeal and swim slowly westward over the dark waters, meeting at last in a sky of broken sun shafts and rose clouds that move silently above a whitened horizon at the end of a perfectly still day.

At such times even the most prosaic, earthbound clam digger is likely to be caught and held by such atmospheric transformations, compelled into some inarticulate response, if only that of pointing his arm to the obvious and omnipresent in a mute gesture of acknowledgment. No drug, no wine, goes to my head like such moments out on the flats. Engulfed by such splendor, I am plucked out of myself like a hermit crab from his borrowed shell and left stranded, naked and unfinished, on the sands.

Scratching is not a prerequisite for experiencing such moments, but it does seem to make them more likely, or at least more intense. It is as though the rhythm and simplicity of the work has a cathartic, purifying effect on my senses, raking and clearing away the accumulated debris of prolonged indoor activity, making me more receptive to outer beauty. In fact, I sometimes suspect that such states of receptivity are my real reason for going clamming, the hidden quarry I may spend an entire afternoon indirectly stalking, the "honey hole" I may by chance stumble on through such physical and mundane labor.

And yet—perhaps because I am so strongly affected by them and seem to spend so much time placing myself in propitious situations in order to catch them—I often ask myself, even while held transfixed in their grip, What good are they, these moments, however beautiful and rare? What does it matter that light and color play in the sky and on the waters, lifting or driving us into states of open-mouthed wonder and a feeling of sudden evisceration? Do such emotions create action or character? Am I really hitched to any deeper life or wider power because of them? Does experiencing them ennoble my behavior or my responses in the human arena? Do I treat my family better or enjoy my real work more because of them? Do they even make me more ready or more sensitive to other, similar moments? I would like to think they do, but it doesn't seem so.

Moreover, such moments can be downright distracting from the work at hand. Sometimes, late in the day when the net of darkness is tightening over the flats, I find I have the choice of topping off my bucket with a few more quahogs or watching the last moments of an October conflagration on the horizon. This may not matter much when the task is essentially recreational, as it is in my case. But what about when the stakes are mortal, as they largely were in the past? I think of the codfisherman of a century ago, hauling in his handline at the coming of night, alone in his fragile shell of a dory on a wide, landless sea. Was he, I wonder, aware of the impeccable sunset flowering like some unexpected dream in the west, and if he was, did he resent and resist the impulse that drew his tired, salt-reddened eyes from his line and threatened to steal the last precious minutes of light from his catch?

Useless, isolated, and distracting they may be; nevertheless nothing can move us more deeply than such moments of intense and unanticipated apprehension. But what is it that we apprehend? What do we think we see? Flames of eternity? Intimations of immortality? Rhythms of creation? In T. S. Eliot's "The Dry Salvages," the poet speaks of experiencing similar moments off Massachusetts's northern cape, Cape Ann, and suggests that they represent "the point of intersection of the timeless with time" or "the moment in and out of time." Is that it? Something genuinely epiphanic, like Emerson's becoming a "transparent eyeball" or Annie Dillard's "tree with lights in it" at Tinker Creek? Do these moments reach beyond the purely physical to something "hidden"? The intensity of our responses may suggest that they do, but for me at least, the actual nature of such experiences, at once overwhelming and ephemeral, will not bear such heavy labels.

Are they, on the other hand, merely physiological? Are we suddenly, simply galvanized by a chance coming together of natural elements that transform us into a kind of bell—a bell rung not by any mystical incarnation but merely by visual and other strictly sensory stimuli, which in turn trigger certain neurochemical and -electric patterns, which in their turn cause us to drop our lower jaws and utter the deity's name? Such a "scientific" explanation may be no more meaningful than any other. In fact, the whole question of beauty may ultimately be no more significant or substantial than that of the number of angels dancing on the head of a pin.

Yet if I had to choose, I would lean toward the latter, more mundane interpretation of these deep and intense moments of natural awareness, not only because it requires no act of faith, but because it strikes me as no less profound or marvelous in its implications than a more transcendental view. It says that our love is not misplaced here on earth, that our sense of wonder and beauty is locked at the very deepest levels into the knotted reality and texture of the physical world from which we wrest a daily living. "The fact," wrote Frost, "is the sweetest dream that labor knows." Who could ask for a more promising vision of life than that? And who would have imagined finding a pearl of such great price in a quahog?

5
___

Scratching is by and large a solitary business. Nonetheless, it is usually when I am out on the flats that I feel most companionable and sociable. Never do I feel so amiably inclined toward my fellow citizens as when I am raking slightly apart from them.

Usually I go out alone, or at most with one or two companions. Frequently I meet friends out on the flats whom I have not seen for months. We smile and say, "Small world," but it isn't really. Rather it is places like this—tidal creeks, herring runs, tern colonies, crab holes, and clam flats—that are the real thoroughfares and gathering places of our community.

We tend to space ourselves out over a broad area and say little while scratching, content to rake apart in silence, with the wind at our backs, drawing the prongs through the soft, gray, muddy sand. What talk there is tends to be of landmarks and seamarks, as though to confirm a sense of where we are out on this wide, unbounded plain. One of us points to a far, dark bar of land to the west, floating like a dead whale on the horizon. "Is that Sandwich?" he shouts. "No, Plymouth," comes the reply. But generally little is said. Wind, light, and space discourage petty conversation, and the tides command our attention.

If we find good digging, we will not move around much but will steadily and methodically reap our own patches of seafloor. The ebb of the tide is our clock, and we ourselves mark its passage as it drops from thigh to knee, knee to calf, until the tops of our wire buckets begin to break above small wavelets and the mounded quahog shells glisten darkly in the nearly horizontal sunlight. As the water falls, the expanse of the Bay drops away from us, leaving each of us alone in a wide, blue field far from land.

This overcrowded peninsula grows increasingly difficult to perceive through its thickening human veneer. Yet out here on these flats I sense there is still space enough for all of us. In the measured rhythm of scratching, in our slow, heavy progress through the water as we move our buckets from place to place, we find an unhurried pace and the sense of a steady, assured, and well-entrenched supply, where every man may go out and find his own limit.

It is getting late. The sky has grown overcast in the course of the afternoon and now grows darker by the minute. I have gotten my limit for the week: ten quarts of chowder quahogs, with perhaps a dozen littlenecks for appetizers. It is time to shoulder my rake and begin the long wade and walk back across the flats to the landing half a mile away.

As I trudge landward, the full, heavy bucket bumps roughly against my waders and grows heavier with each step. This is known as "the quahog's revenge." After a hundred yards or so, I set the bucket down on the hard mud and take a breather. The evening mood is turning all soft and seductive. The gulls laugh softly together on the bars, the low, incoming waters have taken on a silky, saffron color. To the west the strobe-sequined stack of the electric generating plant at the canal spews out a dark, flowing tree of smoke that rises, flattens at the top, and branches out toward the south.

Then, as frequently happens out here at the end of a dull, unremarkable afternoon, the sky explodes with light. The sun drops down out of a shell of dark cloud like a shining, golden yolk and rests for a moment on the horizon, held in a press between earth and sky. Then it falls below the rim of the land and suddenly, as though a switch had been thrown, the whole cowled sky is lit up from beneath, bathing everything in a rosy, diffused glow.

This sudden light gives to the small scattered company of scratchers still out on the flats an unsurpassed intensity of color and outline. Most of them are retired refugees from New Jersey, Long Island, Hartford, or Boston, wearing Swedish rain slickers and wielding rakes made in Parkersburg, West Virginia. But in that moment of searingly pure light I see them in an atavistic posture, an attitude of primitive, intimate contact with the waters surrounding them.

I think of cities I have known, and of the profound loneliness of urban crowds that is the loneliness of a thing unto itself, however large or extensive. True belonging is born of relationships not only to one another but to a place of shared responsibilities and benefits. We love not so much what we have acquired as what we have made and whom we have made it with. There is, at least, the figure for such a love here. And paradoxically, it is in such broad, spacious settings as this—raking the flats, handlining on the banks, working by himself in some common field of endeavor—that a man may feel least alone. The more he allies himself to some varied and interdependent whole, the less he is subject to sudden and wholesale bereavement by chance. His heart rests at the bottom of things; anchored there, he may cast about and never be at sea.

CHAPTER 11

Strandings

You do not expect to see dead animals in the open. It is the nature of animals to die alone, off somewhere, hidden. It is wrong to see them lying out on the highway; it is wrong to see them anywhere.

—LEWIS THOMAS, "Death in the Open"

1
___

Things are beginning to come ashore. This is the time of year for it: mounds of seaweed and eelgrass ripped from the flats, horseshoe crabs and scallop shells stranded on the beach, a numbed and bewildered tropical sea turtle two thousand miles from home, a sick dolphin.

In summer and early fall the shallow, blue waters of the Bay are calm and beguiling, putting on a mask of benignancy for the sun-drenched crowds. But in winter the mask is removed. The Bay is churned into a chilling, gray-green frenzy by stiff northwest winds fetching across forty miles of water from Cape Ann; the long, low protecting curve of its inner shore becomes a hook on which many a fish impales itself, and the cold sea throws up its harvest.

One morning in early December, following a three-day blow, I went down to the Bay shore. The tide was half in. A flock of a few hundred brant flew silently across the outer bars in a long, loose banner, settling near some rocks to feed on eelgrass. Gulls wheeled and skimmed, picking up an occasional clam or scallop.

Along the upper beach the waves and tides of the night before had made new incisions into the bluff and had left a dead harbor seal, about three feet long and virtually unmarked, except for small abrasions on its hide from having been rolled in the surf. Its furry, bullet shape, puppy-dog snout, carefully tucked-under little tail, lay compact and belly up on the sand. A little farther on I found a small ridley sea turtle, slightly more than a foot long with a gray, scuted shell. Marks in the sand suggested that it had been worried and dragged some twenty feet or more up the beach by gulls; its neck lay exposed, red and eaten away. Still farther on I came upon the badly mutilated, almost unrecognizable body of a black duck, with only its head, silver-lined wings, and reddish orange feet left intact for identification. Nearby lay several strands of channeled whelk egg cases. Each strand was composed of about thirty waferlike cases, connected together at their centers to form a sort of pale, wrinkled lei. Each egg case, about the size of a half-dollar, was made of a tough, leathery, translucent material. Breaking one off and holding it up to the sun, I saw inside it the shapes of several dozen unhatched whelks, barely one-eighth of an inch long but completely formed. The miniature shells revealed the dark spots of the embryonic snails within, all doomed to die by desiccation on the beach.

All this I found in less than ten minutes on a winter's morning in a casual survey of a hundred yards or so of beach—not even counting the grass and seaweed lines blown ashore by the winds with whatever smaller life they may have contained. Had I swept the entire, sickle-shaped shore of the Bay that day, who knows what mixed graveyards and nurseries, what frigid fecundity and profligate death, I might have found strewn together?

2
___

One physical aspect of Cape Cod Bay that helps to make it an effective natural trap for a wide variety of marine organisms is its shallowness. The maximum depth of the Bay is about 150 feet, but because of its extensive tidal flats, most inshore areas are only a few fathoms deep. It therefore cools and warms much more rapidly than the surrounding, deeper ocean waters, freezing over regularly in winter and heating up to ninety degrees Fahrenheit or more over some of the flats in summer.

In late fall the Bay waters are subject to periods of sudden cooling. This, coupled with a shift in the prevailing winds to the northwest, often results in some impressive late-season beachings. Floating rafts of moon jellies are blown onto the beaches, to sink and dissolve into the sand. Immature seed scallops, ripped from their eelgrass moorings, are left stranded on the flats, a feast for gulls.

Nearly every winter, beginning in November, one or two dozen southern sea turtles wash up on the Bay shore. These are mostly loggerheads and ridleys, natives of the Caribbean, which in summer wander thousands of miles north of their home waters, carried along by the currents of the Gulf Stream. Numbers of these turtles are found off Cape Cod during the summer and fall months, and many are carried or swim into the warmer waters of the Bay, where they feed on fish, moon snails, and squid. In late fall most begin heading south again, but some, perhaps seduced by the lingering warmth of the Bay and its fall abundance of marine organisms, stay on into November. Being cold-blooded, they are vulnerable to the sudden cooling of the Bay waters at this time of year, which can numb or "cold-stun" them, leaving the turtles to drift helplessly. The strong northwest winds that usually accompany cold fronts then blow them ashore. Some are dead when they land, others slowly die or freeze to death on shore, while a few manage to crawl up the beach and under some vegetation for protection.

Many species of sea turtles have become endangered in recent years owing to overhunting or disturbance of the animals on their tropical breeding beaches. The numbers of ridleys, in particular, have dropped drastically, and no more than five hundred of these turtles are now estimated to be left in the world. A few years ago eight ridleys washed up along the Bay shore during one winter. In recent years, however, sea-turtle watches have been set up here on the Cape and in many other places in New England, and thanks to volunteer efforts many of the stranded turtles have been rescued from the winter beaches and rehabilitated in marine aquariums.

One of the largest, and surely one of the most curious-looking, creatures to fall victim to the Bay's sudden coolings is the ocean sunfish, *Mola mola*. The sunfish looks like some larger-than-life caricature of a fish, an enormous oval hulk that appears to be all head—hence its nickname, "headfish." Two sharklike fins project straight up and down from its huge vertically flattened pancake of a body, while the tail fin has been shortened and modified into a wide, scalloped margin, like the edge of a pie crust. Normally about six feet long, the sunfish reaches a maximum length of ten feet and is covered with an extremely tough, gray, corallike skin, under which is a thick layer of blubber. It has a small, red, horny mouth, a Jimmy Durante nose, and large, staring eyes. Its entire visage is very unfishlike and compellingly human, like something out of *Guernica*, abstract and vulnerable.

Like the sea turtles, ocean sunfish are often found in the Bay in large numbers in late summer and early fall, feeding unhurriedly on jellyfish and comb jellies. They are frequently seen at the surface, where they appear to bask sluggishly in the sun. Like some strange tropical fish grown elephantine and drained of color in our northern waters, the sunfish drifts along through the autumn months, until the Bay swiftly chills, sucking the life out of its unwieldy mass, and it keels over in the surf. Most sunfish that wash ashore are dead, but occasionally one is found alive on the sand, emitting weird moaning sounds that it produces by grating its throat teeth together.

A more common, yet more mysterious, death in Cape Cod Bay is the stranding of large schools of short-finned squid, also called "sea arrows" because of their finned, streamlined shape and remarkable speed. In late fall, for reasons still poorly understood, enormous numbers of these foot-long cephalopods regularly—and apparently intentionally—wash up on our beaches. The most prodigious recent squid stranding occurred in November of 1977 when over ten million short-finned squid came ashore in a series of beachings along the Bay from the Cape Cod Canal to Provincetown.

One day early in the month, just after high tide, I went down to the Bay, where I found their bodies piled up in windrows several feet thick along the windward sides of the stone groins that line the shore. They lay strewn by the thousands, their limp, pale sacks sprouting bouquets of curled and suckered tentacles. Most of the squid seemed to be alive, squirming on the sand or crawling about in shallow tide pools. These were noticeably redder in appearance than the dead ones, with flashes of iridescent color playing across their backs in waves of silent alarm. Like many aquatic organisms, the squid possesses a complex network of contractile chromatophores, enabling it to change color and blend into its background or, possibly, to startle predators by a dazzling display of pulsing hues.

I picked up a live squid out of a tide pool. It turned even redder, as though in anger, latching onto my rubber gloves with its hooked suckers, trying to draw my fingers in toward the black, snapping beak that lay in the center of its writhing rosette of tentacles. Disengaging it with my other hand, I tossed it back out into deeper water. As soon as it left my grasp, it flexed its body sac powerfully, sending several strong jets of water and spurts of black ink shooting through the air. Yet once back in the water the squid showed no impulse to submerge or swim away. Instead, it only bobbed passively at the edge of the tide, and seemed certain soon to be stranded again among its dead and dying companions.

This squid was typical of the millions beached, most of which appeared otherwise healthy and well-fed. Those transported alive to aquariums recovered nicely and were soon swimming about normally in schools. Yet when put back into the water, they never swam offshore; many, in fact, actively tried to beach themselves again.

Several causes have been suggested to explain why these apparently healthy and mobile animals beach themselves in such numbers: disease, parasites, strong winds, cold weather, predators driving them ashore, an instinct to beach after mating, confusion among the squid while chasing food fish across the flats, and periodic population explosions in the Bay which may result in blind dispersals similar to lemming drives in the sub-Arctic. Yet no one cause or combination of them seems to account satisfactorily for the magnitude of these beachings and the puzzling behavior of the individuals involved. Squid strandings seem to lie with the majority of marine deaths in the limbo of the partially explained, that category of phenomena that confuse and frustrate our understanding, not with blank mystery, but with a flood of possible explanations and half-answers, luring us into ever-deeper waters of speculation and hypothesis.

3
_____

Surely the most publicized, and in many ways the most frustrating, of all local strandings are those involving whales, porpoises, and dolphins. During the nineteenth-century the most common marine mammal to beach itself in Cape Cod Bay was the blackfish, or pilot whale, which averages about eighteen feet in length. There exist documented cases of herds of well over a thousand of these animals coming ashore at Provincetown and Truro. Such beachings were welcome windfalls to the local populace, who often set out in small boats to help drive the whales onshore, where they would "try out," or render down, the blackfish blubber in huge iron vats to obtain the valuable whale oil.

When Thoreau witnessed one of these blackfish drives on the Bay side of Truro during the summer of 1855, a local fisherman told him that the whales ran ashore "in pursuit of squid." A century and a quarter later, many cetologists still find this to be as good an answer as any, though many other explanations have been offered in the interim. These include inner-ear parasites that may affect navigation, brain disease causing madness, a racial memory of lost sea channels, man-made pollution, a herd instinct or telepathic imperative to follow a sick or wounded leader, water turbidity or sea-bottom conditions that may interfere with the whales' sonar or echo-location orientation system, even an urge for mass suicide. Though the list is longer and somewhat more sophisticated than that for squid strandings, a near total lack of conclusive evidence marks all of these theories.

Today whale strandings of the magnitude reported a century ago no longer occur in Cape Cod Bay, though pods of up to one hundred blackfish still wash up on occasion. The victims now are more commonly harbor porpoises or white-sided dolphins, either individuals or small groups of half a dozen or less. In many of these cases the causes seem more clear and are thought to be a combination of the Bay's physical properties. Besides being quite shallow near shore, stretches of the Bay's coastline are highly convoluted. Numerous harbors, sandspits, barrier islands, shoals, and marsh creeks create a bewildering labyrinth for large fish and marine mammals feeding inshore. This is particularly true of the oyster flats of Wellfleet Harbor, where the greatest number of marine mammal strandings on the East Coast have occurred. Here the harbor acts as a giant, natural fish weir in which a porpoise or dolphin, lured in on a high tide after smaller food fish, may become confused by the profusion of channels and the turbidity in tidal creeks and thus be stranded on the outgoing tide.

Such "accidental" strandings, however unfortunate, at least appear understandable to us. What is much more frustrating and more difficult to accept are the "voluntary" beachings. Often an apparently healthy whale or dolphin will come ashore. Sympathetic observers, assuming that the animal was driven ashore or caught by outgoing tides, try to push or drag it back into deeper waters. If they succeed, it more often than not turns right around and beaches itself again. It is this "perverse" behavior of stranded whales that has given popular credence to the notion of a racial tendency to suicide.

Part of the problem is that there is still very little statistical information about such voluntary strandings. But another obstacle to our understanding may be that we have been trying to explain such behavior from an anthropomorphic perspective, perhaps because we now regard whales as highly intelligent, and therefore "humanlike," animals. If an intelligent animal in seemingly good health insists on beaching itself, we tend to assume that the act itself is irrational or "suicidal." Yet most cetologists now believe that almost all voluntarily stranded individuals are seriously ill, even dying, however outwardly healthy they may look. It is likely, in fact, that the beachings are motivated not by suicidal tendencies but by the air-breathing mammal's ancient fear of drowning.

A few summers ago, on a hot day in August, a thirty-foot killer whale and her fifteen-foot calf beached on the shallows off Skaket Beach, a popular bathing area at the elbow of the Cape on the Brewster-Orleans line. A concerned crowd managed to push the pair out into deeper water, only to find, to their distress, that the whales soon beached themselves again a short distance to the west. Again the whales were pushed offshore, and again they beached themselves. This scene was repeated several times throughout the afternoon. Each time that a group of bathers and town officials managed to work the two killer whales off the bars and out to deeper water, the mother and calf, with maddening determination, would beach themselves a little farther along the shore. The fire department tried to keep the whales hosed down to prevent their overheating, but it was clear that the pair were becoming exhausted. By sundown the whales had worked their way several miles up the Brewster shore. In one last effort they were pushed offshore and towed several miles out to sea by boat. This time, to everyone's relief, they did not return.

It is very likely, in hindsight, that this humane effort was an act of unintentional cruelty. The killer whales' behavior makes it now seem probable that the female was in considerable distress (she was observed at one time swimming belly up offshore, not the normal position for a healthy killer whale) and was deliberately trying to beach herself. Though she cannot be said to have been consciously seeking aid, and would probably have died anyway, the actions of those on the beach, motivated by admirable sympathy, were more like those of hospital attendants who find a terminally ill patient on their doorstep and call a cab to take her away because she doesn't look sick and might catch a cold lying there.

Two weeks later the carcass of a thirty-foot killer whale was spotted floating several miles out in the Bay. The calf, who may still have been nursing, was never seen again.

4
———

Last November, wanting to gain a better understanding of these beachings, I attended a seminar on marine-mammal strandings given by the New England Aquarium at the Cape

Cod National Seashore headquarters in Wellfleet. By noon, when we broke for lunch, I found myself strangely shaken by what I had seen. The lecture had not been pretty. The aquarium attempts to do complete autopsies on all the carcasses it receives, and the talk had been copiously illustrated with color slides of the autopsy findings. I came away feeling I had attended a police course in homicide rather than a nature lecture, and the slide show was a far cry from the old Walt Disney "True-Life Adventure" movies I had watched as a boy, where the intended victim, it seemed, always got away.

Instead, what we witnessed was an unflinching display of natural pain, sickness, and death. It began with some white-sided dolphins that had stranded in Wellfleet's Herring River that past October. Caught by the treacherous sandbars and outgoing tides, they had thrashed about in a frenzy of escape, cutting themselves to ribbons in the sharp oyster beds. Most had been pregnant females, near full term, with, as the lecturer put it, "every reason to live." Some had open "shotgun" wounds where the opportunistic gulls had attacked the fatty pouches just below their eyes.

If such stranded animals do not get eaten alive or bleed to death first, they usually die of heat prostration. Their natural blubber insulation and dark coloration, which help them gather and retain body heat in the cold seas, serve to bake them to death on land.

From these we passed on to instances of apparently intentional beachings which make up the great majority of individual strandings. Though the motivations for such strandings are still in doubt, the cause of death in each case can usually be determined by an autopsy. A beached animal may appear quite healthy because its injuries and infections are often internal and because marine mammals have what one researcher called "great staying power," or what we might call stamina, endurance, the will to live. But it is also "staying power" in the literal sense, for, as was pointed out, a sick dolphin cannot go to bed to recuperate but must *stay* up with the herd or die. By the time such animals beach, therefore, most are as good as dead. Of *all* voluntarily stranded cetaceans, only two are known to have survived and recovered. Those that were shown to us made me wonder how most even managed to make it to shore alive.

We watched slides of brain lesions, caused by aberrant parasites, that can paralyze one half of a dolphin so that it swims futilely in circles until, finally exhausted, it sinks or strands. Other cetaceans had massive infections of nematode worms. The best-known of these is a species that affects the middle ears of blackfish and is thought to interfere with the animals' hearing and navigational equipment. Other worms, looking like twisted masses of spaghetti, clogged the animals' sinus passages, lungs, and heart vessels, slowing them down, strangling them from inside until they could no longer catch food or keep up with the herd.

Certain parasitic worms are known to concentrate in the mammary glands of porpoises. Slides of mother's milk taken from infected pregnant females showed it riddled with worm eggs, suggesting the pretty probability that this parasite is transmitted during nursing.

One particularly grisly slide showed a white-sided dolphin body stripped of its blubber layer during an autopsy. The bloody carcass was nearly entirely encrusted with what looked like white barnacles. It was explained that these were the encysted forms of a tapeworm that usually uses the dolphin as an intermediate host. The adult form of the tapeworm is found in sharks; it presumably gets there by way of a piece of dolphin meat. Adult worms lay eggs in the sharks. These are voided and picked up by scavenger animals, which in turn are eaten by the dolphins. At first such an arrangement might seem a bit chancy for the worms. But few dolphins in the ocean die of old age, and the alternatives to stranding are limited. The worm's bet is, after all, a pretty good one.

In the pinnipeds, or seal and walrus family, it is the juveniles, seven to eleven months old, that suffer the greatest mortality, usually during their first winter. During the winter of 1974–75, eighty young harbor seals washed up in the Bay, all dead of natural causes. We saw seal bodies covered with viral eruptions and bacterial lesions; also copious examples of protozoan, heartworm, and lungworm infection that, as in dolphins, slow the seals down so that they are not able to catch food. Since a seal depends primarily on the fish it eats for its freshwater needs, these infected youngsters may die of dehydration before starvation, exhaustion, or killer whales can overtake them.

Malnutrition and vitamin deficiency in young seals can also cause severe pyorrhea, or gum recession. Many of those we saw had lost several teeth. One animal, whose infection had become so bad that the jawbone itself was exposed, had been mercifully anesthetized by the aquarium staff. Often these young seals come ashore with what look like serious head injuries, mistakenly attributed to human clubbing. These are actually the result of massive infestations of seal "lice," minute blood-sucking crustaceans whose numerous tiny punctures give the seal's head its bloody appearance.

I came out of the lecture and into the midday air, moved in some vague, unanticipated way. It was not so much the gory nature of the slides that disturbed me (though the suggestion to break for an early lunch was lukewarmly received by most of us) as the terrible *earnestness* of life they had conveyed. I had thought I knew something about the reality of survival in the wild, but this was more than I had bargained for and it gave me a momentary loss of bearings.

I wandered away from the building and out across the barren plain of old Camp Wellfleet, an army base during World War II, out to the ocean bluff, where the sea rocked equitably below me. There were no mutilated bodies on the beach today.

The wind, though coming out of the north, was not yet raw and harsh, and I could see no malice in the surf.

Still, I found myself asking, What am I to make of a world where an animal like the dolphin—intelligent, communicative, graceful in form and rapid in movement, in many ways our aquatic counterpart—is from a worm's point of view merely a resting place on its way to a shark's belly, where whale calves suck death with their mother's milk, and where the faces of young seals turn into grinning, bloody death's heads?

Even as I silently voiced this protest, however, I knew it represented no serious philosophical problem but was merely a defense mechanism. We would devoutly like nature to reflect the consideration and concern that we have managed to wrest to such a tenuous degree for ourselves. A sense of fair play is a human invention that, however admirable, has not yet made the rest of the universe beat a path to our door. Dying of old age, in relative painlessness, surrounded by affectionate, caring companions is not only a still-uncommon occurrence among humanity but also a freakish anomaly among living things as a whole.

Despite our intellectual acceptance of the principle of indifference in nature, we are not yet so far from our unshielded past that we can afford to look nakedly at life in the wild for very long. We dare not examine our belief in the sacredness of life too closely in the bleak light of natural mortality, lest the world seem unbearably profane, and we are thrown back on dark religions. So we hide death where we can, leaving it to police or doctors, or soft-pedal it in our edited renderings of the natural world.

It is comparatively easy to do this inland, where nature itself seems to abet us in the conspiracy. Lewis Thomas marveled that he had lived all his life with "an embarrassment of squirrels" in his backyard, yet had never seen a dead one. For better or worse, such a view is more difficult here. The land may cloak its deaths in blankets of leaves and quick decomposition, but the ocean, less decorous than honest, throws up its casualties to view, at times so candidly and in such numbers, however, that we seem to live on a sinking island of life surrounded by a vast morgue.

5

In contrast to the baffling "beaching instinct" of so many marine organisms and the questionable value of our own efforts to help them, observers have long noted and admired the cetacean trait of giving aid and protection to weak or injured members of their own species, and occasionally to human swimmers as well, even at risk to themselves. An example of this was witnessed here a few years ago when three white-sided dolphins swam in from the Bay into Quivett Creek in West Brewster. Two of the dolphins were apparently helping the third one, which was sick or hurt, keeping it buoyed up above the surface and attempting to move it into the shallower and calmer waters of the tidal creek. The result of this seemingly altruistic behavior was that all three dolphins were stranded on the outgoing tide and died.

In *A Natural History of Marine Mammals* Victor B. Shaeffer discusses such observed behavior as a "care-giving instinct" that, despite such ironic results, has "survival value" to the species as a whole. Describing what appear to us to be deliberately compassionate acts in terms of "instinct," or calculating its value in mathematical percentages of gene survival, may seem cold and mechanistic, but perhaps it is not. Perhaps the dolphins, whose brains are at least the equivalent of ours in size and complexity, are smart not to be more intelligent than they are—if awareness of one's motives constitutes intelligence. In their unsparing world of the ocean, too much knowledge may be a mistake, too much conscious compassion a liability. Having learned something about what these animals are up against, I found myself wondering just how much of a "kindness" it really is to attempt to save them (even when we think we know what we are doing), only to return them to such a stark and unmitigated existence. Are we perhaps not still seeing them too much as reflections of ourselves, their misery as cloaked perceptions of our own pitiless and vulnerable state?

Yet we really have no choice but to try. All of those individuals and institutions that spend so much time, effort, and expense trying to help and understand these stricken animals—whether beached whales, benumbed turtles, or diseased seals—are not merely after a greater knowledge of their life history, biochemistry, or population dynamics (though these things are essential to conservation efforts). They also care for them as fellow creatures, easing their pain where they can and, however slim the chances of success, working for their recovery.

Perhaps in a way we are even more vulnerable than these naked creatures, for we are liable to die of grief as well as brain lesions and heartworms. We risk "care-giving" beyond any traceable instinct, into the conscious investment of personal affection and concern for the welfare not only of other human beings but also for the other forms of life with which we share this planet. Such behavior on our part may ultimately have "survival value" to us as a species, ensuring a healthy and varied environment. But it may go beyond even enlightened self-interest and scientific curiosity. I think we cannot help it. In spite of the risks that such caring involves, it is part of our emotional and psychological makeup, part of being human.

One thing is certain: marine mammals, whose ancestors were terrestrial, did not return to life in the sea because it was any easier there than on land. If anything, life in the sea is in many ways harsher and more precarious. Just so, our broadening compassion for life at large does not necessarily make our lives any easier. As with the dolphins, it is part of our evolution as a species. Like them, we possess a staying power against all odds. In our case it stems from an inextinguishable belief in life and its ultimate value—a belief that is sustained in part by life's own ability to produce such water-borne shapes of unsurpassed beauty, leaping above the dark waves, shattering sunlight on broad, glistening backs, before crashing down again into cold, callous seas.

CHAPTER 12

Ice in the Bay

1

When the Bay finally freezes over, as it does nearly every winter, there is almost a feeling of relief, as though a white sheet were mercifully thrown over the all-too-visible leavings of the shore.

One calm morning in mid-January, mild and sunny, I went down to the Bay shore, where a wide rim of broken ice already stretched out over a hundred yards from the beach. By the end of the month, it would spread well beyond sight, but already the silence of the shoreline was arresting, even a bit appalling.

Sounds were few, stark, isolated, and heightened: the distant yodel of a gull; a dog's barking, obsessed and maniacal. The gulls themselves were spread out here and there on the ice field, standing with stupid, curious stares. For the most part they remained still and quiet, as though their usual clamoring and gliding, from which not even the fiercest gales deter them, had been quelled by the strange calm around them. Out on the far edge of the ice, through my binoculars, I saw a large blackback methodically picking apart one of its dead companions.

The silence was arctic and engulfing, despite the mildness of the day. It shed a perfect, poised stillness over everything, like the predawn calm on a lake in summer, or the quailed resignation of a desert at noon, yet different from either and carrying a sense of heightened expectation in this place of constant flux.

The ice itself, though for the most part a chaotic and porous jumble, made no noise. If I listened intently, though, I could hear, far out at the edge of the thin skim ice, a soft susurrus, like the rustling of silk; and farther in, small squeaking noises, like cabinet hinges needing oil, made by the pulse of stifled waves beneath the firmer ice. No sound of movement, however, reached the hard, four-foot shelf of tide-piled ice that layered the shore.

As I walked east, the ice gradually spread farther out, as though I were walking deeper and deeper into winter. Bay ice is generally thickest as one approaches the inner elbow of the Cape, where the prevailing winds and longshore currents pack it in like snow into the corner of a windowpane. At the Brewster-Orleans line it is often well over a mile wide and can look convincingly permanent.

I stopped and walked out onto one of the larger rock groins, which still raised its bouldered back above the ice, like the carapace of some enormous sea turtle breaking out of a white sea. Stepping gingerly out across the slippery stones, I surveyed the barren majesty of the Bay. Salt ice here is never a smooth, seamless cover like that which forms on our lakes and ponds, but like the earth's crust, it is a mosaic of plates, solid in themselves, but still subject to movement by the hidden tides. Like old people who have lost their flexibility yet are forced to change in a cold, accelerating world, the ice ruptures in the process, creating numerous cracks and rifts. One of these rifts appeared before me now just beyond the end of the groin, a thin, dark crack that within minutes widened to a green, icy river several yards wide. There, floating by in its exhumed currents was a steady and seemingly endless stream of flotsam: gull feathers, goose turds, several dead or torpid fish, what looked like a seal's flipper, several plastic bottles, a child's doll.

2

Though the ice in the Bay halts the tides of marine strandings and even to some degree protects the beach from erosion by winter storms, it may, if severe and prolonged enough, eventually begin to produce a death of its own. In the grip of an extended winter freeze on the Bay, the main victims tend to be not marine organisms but birds.

During the winter of 1976–77 most of the bays and estuaries of Cape Cod remained solidly iced over for five weeks. By mid-December the cold had frozen even the largest of our fresh-water ponds, driving their winter populations of black ducks and mergansers out into the Bay to join the sea ducks and brant. By New Year's Day the marshes and coastal waters had become locked in as well. Many of the smaller waterfowl, unfit for the rough weather of the open ocean, began congregating in the remaining bits of open water near the shore—springs, creeks, and tidal races—as we once huddled about dwindling fires.

In the lower reaches of Stony Brook Valley, where Paine's Creek runs beside the state highway, I watched for a week the fortunes of five small horned grebes that had taken refuge there. As the days progressed and the cold deepened, the ice crept down off the peat banks of the marsh and out into the tidal creek, gradually narrowing it down to a thin and broken thread of open, icy water. On Friday morning I found the grebes huddled in a single remaining patch of water less than four feet across, near the road. Their lives had been whittled down to this one small opening against the encroaching ice, an opening so small it was conceivable that only their collective body heat was keeping it open.

They evinced no desperation, but I knew that if the hole closed in the night, as it was almost certain to do, they had nowhere to go. Grebes, like loons and pelagic seabirds, are built for open water and have great difficulty taking off from land (or ice), even when not weakened from hunger, as these very likely were. By taking refuge here, they had, so to speak, painted themselves into a corner. But they had made their choice and must stick it out. Were they at all aware that their lives hung in the balance of a night? For me, their tenacious presence added a new element of risk and daring to this little brook.

Later that day, by a capricious turn in the weather, the sun warmed and the afternoon tide came in, breaking up the creek ice for a few hours. Perhaps the grebes realized after all what a tight spot they had been in, for the next morning they were gone.

Other waterfowl were not so fortunate. The critical problem for most wintering species is the lack not of open water but of food. The marshes and eelgrass flats are their primary food sources, and these had been cut off by the ice. Most birds, having eaten well throughout the fall, can survive two or three weeks on little or no nourishment. When a deep freeze comes, some migrate southward; but most stay on, for experience has taught them that they can endure normal periods of ice in the Bay.

As January continued, however, there were increasing signs that this was no ordinary freeze. Numbers of waterfowl began to approach the edge of extremity. Brant, normally very wary birds, were spotted grazing on the fairways of local golf courses. A friend of mine encountered an eider duck on the shore, creeping up the beach directly toward him, as though asking to be taken in out of the cold. Several dead and dying herons were found on the frozen marshes. One of these, an emaciated great blue heron, was brought to the Cape Cod Museum of Natural History and placed in the furnace room for warmth. It was so weak from starvation that it could barely stand. As I approached it, the heron tottered backward and collapsed angularly to the cement floor like a giant folding rule, though it kept its undaunted eyes and large yellow bill pointed warningly in my direction. I saw that its yellow, scaly feet were mere stubs, looking as though something had gnawed them off. The long claws and the first two joints on each toe were missing, probably the result of extended or repeated frostbite. But the injuries appeared to be old ones and had healed over. Apparently the bird had managed to stalk and spear its prey on these blackened stubs for some time, perhaps for years, until all chance for prey had disappeared for good beneath white, impregnable armor.

By far the hardest-hit species during that winter were the Canada geese, in part because they winter here in such large numbers, particularly in the marshes at the elbow of the Cape, where the ice buildup was greatest. Their forage here is almost entirely water vegetation—marsh grass, rush roots, eelgrass—and they had little recourse once these sources were shut off. Migration was now their only chance, but most had become too weakened by hunger to attempt it. Their strategy of waiting it out was proving fatal.

By the third week of the freeze, the bodies of several dozen dead geese littered the frozen surfaces of nearby marshes and bays. I examined one that I found in Quivett Creek, running my hand along the sleek, black feathers of its long, slim neck, prodding the soft, white mound of chest feathers. There was almost nothing there. The strong pectoral muscles that had carried the goose down from its northern nesting grounds late last fall had been reduced to stringy remains, still attached to the large, protruding keel bone.

As the long winter wore on and stress piled upon stress, it became increasingly difficult to distinguish between natural and man-made death. In addition to the ice and cold, the Cape's waters were hit by a series of major oil spills, the largest by far being the grounding of the oil tanker *Argo Merchant* on December 21 on the Nantucket Shoals. The ship split in half in heavy seas, dumping some 7.5 million gallons of crude oil into the Atlantic just a few miles offshore. The steady northwest winds that were keeping the Bay frozen also kept the oil from reaching the ocean beaches, but an undetermined number of seabirds were fouled by the spreading slicks. Over forty murres, auks, loons, gannets, eiders, and gulls were recovered on the beaches and brought to our museum for cleaning. Through the heroic efforts of staff members, one out of three birds survived, but only those that made it to shore alive were recovered to begin with. It was estimated that for every oiled bird that reached land, ten did not.

3
___

Most of the dead animals brought to the museum in winter are piled outside near the back entrance—in a kind of natural freezer. The driveway to this rear entrance, used by museum employees, is marked with a sign that says "Handicapped Only," which has given much amusement to the staff in the past. During the long freeze, however, the approach was strewn not only with the handicapped but also with the maimed, the battered, the starved, the diseased, and the dead of the natural world: piles of emaciated geese, oiled alcids dead of pneumonia, herons without their feet, gulls with broken wings, a three-foot loggerhead turtle with one leg chewed off, an unmarked harbor porpoise whose smooth rubbery skin looked synthetic, unreal, as though it were a plastic model of itself.

One Sunday morning in early February, when the museum

was closed, I drove up to the back entrance, intending to get a book I needed from the library. I made my way quickly past the mounds of frozen carcasses beside the rear door and let myself in to the deserted building. Inside, it was dim and strangely quiet. I walked down the long carpeted hallway toward the library but was stopped by some gurgling noises that seemed to be coming from inside a large plastic garbage can set at the head of the stairs leading to the basement. I lifted the lid and peered inside. At the bottom I could make out the indistinct form of a duck—a scaup, it seemed—lying flat on its stomach. Its head and neck were stretched out on some straw bedding, and it was breathing with difficulty. Near its bill some grain had been scattered, which had not been touched, and pools of pale, runny excrement trailed out behind its tail.

Poor, ravaged bird! It looked like some travesty of the life process, though its yellow-black eyes glared steadily and defiantly up at me in its extremity. As I stooped down for a closer look, the scaup began coughing and wheezing, huffing with excitement, though it could not even manage to raise its neck. At last I kneeled down beside it, and for several minutes stayed there, just stroking its bony, exhausted body and staring back at those cold, yellow eyes. Then all at once a deep chill began to spread through my limbs. It seemed to be growing terribly dark and cold around me. I felt the life draining out of me and into this dying bird, and was suddenly frightened to the bone. Forcing myself to my feet, I fled the building, forgetting what I had come for.

4
————

This winter beach, glazed with a rim of death, is itself a kind of entrance for the "handicapped only," where the injured, the moribund, and the dead are wheeled up its frozen ramp by the serviceable tides for our inspection. It is no doubt a needed corrective to all our neat, healthy, well-lit aquariums, to our smiling summer sands and our long, mild autumns, which sometimes lull us into half believing that the weather has lost its earnestness and winter has gone out of fashion for good. Such chilly scenes remind us that life is still in the minority.

And yet we who come to the world through such back entrances may ourselves come away somewhat handicapped in our sensibilities and crippled in our expectations. It is, in the end, not the unflinching display of casualties here, not the openness of their dying or the pitiful, raw nakedness of their suffering, not even our own helplessness in the face of such things, that eventually catches us off guard and makes us flee blindly back to our garrisons of life. Rather, it is the simple unexceptionability of such deaths.

Here, at the sea's edge, we tend to focus on the large and visible—ten million squid, a thousand blackfish, a nursing killer whale, hundreds of starving birds—which easily claim our attention and sympathy. We discuss and analyze "mysterious" die-offs, "inexplicable" strandings, and "unprecedented" freezes, describing them as "accidents," "freak epidemics," and "tragedies"—and so at last mislead ourselves into believing that there is really something extraordinary about all this dying.

Yet on any ebb tide, at any season, the flats and beaches are strewn with the debris of life. Look down at your feet and you will see, in the grooved and ripples of the sand, the bleached shells of whelks, the cracked carapaces of calico and green crabs, the dismembered claws of jonah crabs, the rent ribbons and fronds of kelp, rockweed, and bladder wrack, empty scallop shells, small white surf clams, and iridescent fish scales.

Farther in, higher up on the beach, is the rich wreckage of the wrack line: mounds of eelgrass studded with moon snails, periwinkles, and slipper shells, the fried remains of moon jellies, and the amputated appendages of dead-man's-fingers, worm-bored and barnacle encrusted pieces of driftwood, the stately or storm-smashed bodies of waterfowl and shorebirds—and everywhere uncountable gull feathers and the shells of horseshoe crabs, strewn across the sands like the fallen flags and shattered shields of some gallant and impersonal defeat.

Even on the calmest, mildest days, when the rhythm of the tide slides in and out, noiselessly and without breaking, the highest reaches of the beach are laced with delicate, black tracings of wrack, pulverized grist from the sea's mills. This finest of all wrack is composed of minutely ground bits of seaweed, shells, crustacean skeletons, and other organic remains crushed beyond identification. Once, examining some of these thin, looping necklaces of sea dust, I saw that they were strung with innumerable empty shells of a tiny bivalve mollusk known as *Gemma gemma*, the gem clam. They are roughly triangular in shape and have a beautiful mother-of-pearl coating tinted with purple and finely crenulated inside edges. I picked one up—it was only an eighth of an inch across—and saw that the shell was pierced with the perfectly beveled hole of a predatory oyster drill.

5

The ice is breaking up in the Bay. The long freeze finally began to relax its grip in early February. By midmonth the marshes and smaller estuaries unlocked to the point where the geese and other waterfowl could begin feeding again. The piles of carcasses outside the museum began to diminish, though there would be many more oil-spill victims before the long winter was finally over.

Then a week of warming weather, high tides, and easterly gales tore the Bay apart. Almost overnight the flats at low tide became a scene of massive desolation scattered with enormous, stranded floes of ice that looked like the ruins of a thousand Stonehenges, megaliths of a race of giants that had withdrawn and vanished with the tides. I walked among them and peered into their dark, cavelike openings, dripping and shaggy with trapped clumps of uprooted marsh grass.

Now the ice disgorged its dead: creek minnows and larger fish, half thawed and drooping out of the soft, rotten, icy walls; the mashed and darkened bodies of black ducks and herring gulls, hidden for weeks in the dark crevices, now exhumed and open to view; and great mounds of scallop shells, scooped and swept into twenty-foot depressions of the ice's making, like bodies heaped into shallow graves.

But it is over. The ice has retreated. There will be more cold spells, more deaths, perhaps even more blizzards, but it will never again be like this—not this winter.

One evening in late February, after the last of the ice had disappeared, I went down to the shore to see what the darkness and the water had to offer. The night was damp and warm, and the rain soughed against my back in gentle gusts of wind like snow off pine boughs. At the water's edge the tide was an hour or two past high. Dark and thick with torn seaweed, it lisped angrily at the beach. Not much to be found here tonight, I thought, almost in gratitude.

Then I shone my flashlight along the beach and saw that the wrack line was studded with numerous, glistening, black objects the size of eggs. They were eggs—or skate egg cases, to be exact, commonly known as mermaid's or sea purses. For as far as I could see, they littered the night beach in an unbroken line. I had found skate cases many times before, mostly in summer, but never had I seen them in such quantity. In the half-mile or so of beach that I walked, there were two or three every foot, and when I finally turned back, their numbers showed no signs of abating. Sea purses—what a spending there was that night!

Skates are primitive, cartilaginous fish, smaller relatives of sharks and rays, whose pectoral fins are fused together into broad "wings," giving them a flattened, fanlike shape. There are two common species of skates in Cape Cod Bay; these egg cases were most likely those of the winter skate, *Raja ocellata*, so called because it prefers colder water and is found close to shore on the Massachusetts coast only during winter months. Each case is rectangular in shape, with two pairs of tentacles, or "horns," unequal in length, coming off opposite ends; and each, when laid, contains a single fertilized egg.

Despite their unusual appearance, these egg capsules are ingeniously contrived structures. Composed of keratin, a tough, horny substance that also forms our fingernails, each case forms around the embryo only hours before it is deposited by the female skate. The whiplike horns at each end are curved and coated with a gummy substance to catch on seaweeds or shells on the sea bottom.

Though they contain marine fish, skate egg cases are waterproof, for saltwater is initially fatal to a developing embryo. At the end of about three weeks, however, the skate embryo has used up the albumen that has been plugging small holes in the tips of the horns, and seawater begins to seep in. Now supplied with gills, the tiny skate pumps in the oxygen-laden water at one horn opening by swishing its tail back and forth, and expels it out of the other three holes, like some self-contained heart. At the end of nine or ten weeks, the purse end near the longer pair of horns splits and the young skate emerges, wings folded, like a butterfly out of its cocoon. A flick of its tail and it is free of the case, launched into the wide sea.

The purses that shone in my light were mostly greenish black, sometimes iodine, in color, with a grained texture. All that I picked up were empty; all had the telltale slit of escape at one end. Of the hundreds of skate egg cases I have examined over the years, never have I found a dead embryo inside any. The newly emerged skate, like most marine young, has only a slim chance of living to adulthood; and yet the windrows of empty cases I found that evening at least attested to the vigorous start they receive in their run for survival.

And what if the egg cases had not been empty? Would the message have been any different? Are not all the stranded and dead forms on this shore egg cases as well: empty containers and mangled husks from which the life has flown? Moreover, does not their visible and often overwhelming presence stand as testimony, not just to the universality of death and the harshness of existence, but even more to the persistence and endurance of life in the face of such unmitigable conditions?

After all, if we know life in part from our acquaintance with death, we know death *solely* from the life it harvests, as we know time from the deterioration it brings. How much more barren, morbid, and ultimately terrifying would this beach be without its mangled and mutilated bodies? How much more anxious would I be about the status of all unseen life if I found no extinguished or discarded signs of its continuity? If death suddenly ceased along this shore, where would life be? Death is the stranded testament of life in these waters, and with it earth and sea create their endless, unsentimental poetry. In the rain and darkness the black, shining mermaid's purses stretched out along the winter beach in an endless line of birth and renewal, empty tokens of a rich and abiding dispensation.

CHAPTER 13

The Landing

1
———

Last night I stood at the landing at Paine's Creek and listened to the alewives come in. It was just dusk when I arrived, and in the dying light the exposed flats were veined with black, shining water. An old cart track still wound its way through the newly greening cord grass of the fringe marsh along the shore, and beyond, on the flats, hundreds of gulls sat on the edges of the outflowing stream channel or paddled lazily in its shallow current. Some of the birds flew up when I got out of the car, wheeling and screaming like large, fragmented wings against the rosy afterlight of the sunken sun, ashes rising from the watery grave of the day's fire.

As I walked out along the cart track toward the creek delta, I became aware of a flapping, swishing sound in the running waters of the stream beside me. It sounded like waves sucking back over a pebbled beach, but the creek bed here has no pebbles in it, only sand. In the thickening darkness, I could see nothing but water and decided that it must be the voice of Stony Brook itself (or rather, of its lower-half identity, Paine's Creek)—the loose, flapping tongues of sand and water flopping over upon themselves in the shallow ripples and swift outrunning current.

But a curious rhythm and respiration in the sound, coupled with a sudden urgency and movement toward the shore by the gulls, sent me back to the car for a flashlight. Shining it out over the creek waters, I saw the white, slithering forms, edged in black, of running alewives, burrowing their way across the shallow entrance bars of the creek. Here the outflowing waters drove up into a turbulence that was but a few inches deep and must have been nearly as much sand as water. But the fish came on, in hordes, like rounded riffles in a mountain stream, with a persistence that seemed to say they did not care what substance or what texture they had to navigate. Water, sand, air—it did not matter, so long as it would support their bodies and give passage. I felt they would have gone through snow, if that was what they had encountered there.

I had been right. It was the voice of the stream I heard, though not of Stony Brook or Paine's Creek or any of the individual local identities assigned to it by white men or Indians over the centuries in which both men and fish had trafficked in its waters. That night at the landing the alewives proclaimed it a more basic identity, one it shares in fecund anonymity with scores of similar streams up and down this coast. I stood in the dark and listened to the many-finned, many-tongued voice of Herring River.

2

The town landing at Paine's Creek is about two miles from my house, on the east side of the creek mouth. Use of the landing goes back far into the town's history. Old records refer to a seventeenth-century tidal mill somewhere in the vicinity, but its exact location and function are not known. Shore fishermen and lobstermen have always moored their small skiffs and catboats in the shelter of the creek. In the late 1800s, when larger boats out of deeper harbors caused a decline in local offshore fishing, numerous fish weirs festooned the flats with their intricate mazes of nets and poles. Men set out from the creek mouth in skiffs to tend these weir traps at high tide, and at low tide drove horse-drawn, sky blue, wide-wheeled wagons from the landing out onto the flats where they gathered their harvests of cod, mackerel, bass, and an occasional tuna, pitchforking fragrant piles of fish on the wagons as high as hay loads.

Business was brisk enough around the turn of the century that a wooden fish house was built on the east side of the landing road. But because of the long stretch of flats between the creek mouth and deep water, Paine's Creek was never dredged out to accommodate larger boats. This lack of a ship harbor has always grated on the inhabitants of Brewster, and there have been various efforts over the years to enlist federal and state help to create one, but to no avail. As recently as 1976, the board of selectmen, chagrined that Brewster was "the only town on Cape Cod without a marina," submitted a proposal to the U.S. Army Corps of Engineers to study the feasibility of dredging a harbor and boat channel in the vicinity of Paine's Creek. Even the redoubtable Corps, however, balked at the necessity of dredging a three-mile channel to reach deep water, and it returned an unfavorable report.

One of the few old houses in town built on the shore sits on a rise just behind the landing. Constructed about 1850 by Augustus Paine, it is a large, handsome, two-story structure of the period with several gables and two tall, thin brick chimneys. Directly west of the creek is Wing's Island, a twenty-acre deposit of glacial till surrounded by salt marsh that was the site of a house built in 1656 by John Wing, the first white settler in Brewster. In the early nineteenth century several saltworks (a widespread Cape industry that obtained salt from seawater by pumping it by means of windmills into large evaporating sheds) were operated on the island, and occasionally one still comes upon one of the old wooden pipes—a hollowed-out log of cedar or pine—lying high up on the marsh, crevassed and silvered with time. After the town bought Wing's Island, in 1964, an ambitious selectman had a wooden footbridge constructed to it across Paine's Creek from the landing. The bridge mysteriously burned shortly after it was completed, however, and no attempt to replace it has been made since.

The old fish house, the weir traps, the saltworks, the commercial fishermen and lobstermen, the wooden skiffs, and the sky blue wagons are all gone now. A few sailboats and small motorboats still moor in the creek during the summer months, and at high tide in July and August the landing is one of the busiest of our small town beaches, jammed with cars and people. But the setting itself—the long, low, braided mosaic of marsh, creek, low dunes, and wide flats—remains, after centuries of use and continued attempts at alteration, one of the most unspoiled and inviting stretches of beach along the entire Bay shore.

3

At all times of the year, the landing is a place where people and animals congregate, residents and seasonal visitors alike, for a variety of needs and purposes. It draws, like a magnet, fish and swimmer, gull and clammer, shorebirds and sunbathers. It is both an end and a beginning for journeys, a resting place and a point of departure, an escape and a challenge.

During the summer months terns join the gulls at the creek mouth, grazing the waters as they hunt for sand eels in the shallows, or fluttering and diving to spear a minnow in the deeper channels of the marsh. By July the young herring fry, barely two inches long, are carried down from the mill ponds and mix by the millions in the creek's lower waters, glancing against and tickling the calves and ankles of summer waders as the tiny fish are swept out to sea.

In late summer and autumn, flocks of tree swallows, sand-pipers, and plovers migrate along the beach, feeding in the fringe marsh that fronts the landing, while a loose parade of monarch butterflies flutters over the dunes, bound for Mexico. Occasionally large schools of menhaden, another member of the herring family, are driven ashore by predating bluefish. The smaller fish attempt to take shelter in the creek mouth and are left stranded and gull gored by the hundreds on the receding tide, while the voracious bluefish, biting at anything in their frenzy of appetite, attract dozens of surf casters to the landing to participate in and profit by the general slaughter.

The landing beach receives its share of late-autumn strand-ings, and in deep winter, when the ponds are frozen and pack ice cakes the Bay beyond sight, the creek mouth will remain open in all but the severest freezes, providing a small haven and source of food for black ducks, brant, herons, and other waterfowl. Even when the creek closes over, the gulls remain, constant buffers to the wind.

Not too many years ago there must have been times when the landing remained deserted for days on end, not only because far fewer people lived in the town, but because the means of getting there were not so universally available. In the past, life was no less grim here, but the unemployed, the unrequited, the merely restless, and the sick at heart had to nurse their wounds at home. They could not always, as we can, jump in a car and wind down to the land's gentle end where, sensing an appeal beyond the human community, they might share their grief with the tide.

Now, however, the landing serves year-round human needs, beyond the recreational demands of the sprawling summer crowds. Even on the bleakest, rawest winter days, I can rarely spend an hour there without another car pulling up beside me. It is a place to walk, to run your dog, to take a nap, eat lunch, take the kids, take a break, read the paper, talk things out, make out, split up, gather eelgrass off the beach for garden mulch, watch a storm or fireworks or the northern lights across the Bay, see a sunset or, more rarely, a sunrise.

People come in cars and trucks, by boat, on motorcycles and bicycles, pushing baby carriages and walking their dogs. Some, like the dog walkers, show up regular as clockwork, regardless of weather. Others roar in briefly, race their motors impatiently several times, and then, as though they had come down the wrong street, roar off again.

Occasionally an entire family lumbers down to the landing in a large trailer camper that nearly fills the small parking lot. Eating dinner inside, they watch the tide through a picture window, as though on television, running out to meet an impeccable sunset. A few summer visitors, finding the local campgrounds and motels full, try to spend the night there, only to be informed of the town's anticamping bylaw by the local police cruiser at 2 A.M.

The advantages of a place like this are usually listed in narrow recreational terms: swimming, boating, shellfishing, and the like, but the landing serves community functions that do not ordinarily show up on federal or state coastal-resource inventories. From its asphalted platform I have watched herring race up the creek to spawn, seen a hundred kites and a score of romances launched, observed terns diving for eels and a snow bunting plucked on the wing from the midst of its flock by the dark, twisting form of a pigeon hawk, witnessed the angry, tearful ends of marriages and the first, tentative steps of infants in the sand. It is not unlikely that more than one resident has been conceived or has died here.

Deliverymen, garbagemen, plumbers, carpenters, electricians, salesmen, highway-crew workers, shopping housewives, and others on the road make short detours to the landing

at all hours of the day for five-minute "rut breaks." I sometimes think that simply knowing that such places exist, even if
we do not always take advantage of them, adds to the psychological well-being of the community as a whole.

I myself have gone to the landing for its therapeutic value
on more than one occasion. Usually it is after some seemingly
endless committee meeting or public hearing, when my brain
feels polluted and my mouth tastes of dust and cotton from too
much pointless talking. Driving home, I unconsciously turn
off the highway and swing down toward the Bay. Reaching
the unlighted landing at the bottom of the road, I switch off
the lights, and there before me stretches the dark, beckoning
plain of the flats, full of pungent smells, wandering cries, and
the resurgent, far-off growl of the incoming tide: voices, entities, and elements all wandering in honest solitude. Near the
shore a night heron detaches itself from one of the dark clumps
of marsh grass and calls out in surly querulousness, a genuine
note that answers the evening.

People, it seems, are less inhibited in their behavior and with
their emotions on a beach, as though they sense that life moves
on a more open and tolerant scale here and human judgments
are less compelling. (Curiously, one often gets the same
impression in the middle of a large city.) Old men come and
fall asleep in their cars, large, grandmotherly women yell in
coarse language at their dogs, and young couples grapple
unselfconsciously in the sand.

The night, especially, seems to bring out uncommon behavior. One summer evening I encountered a young man on the
beach at the landing, dressed only in cut-off denims and
engaged in some kind of Zen exercise, moving his limbs in the
imperceptibly slow and controlled motions of ritualistic dance.
Though we were the only ones on the beach and though I
passed within five feet of him, he took no more notice of me
than he would if I had been a mushroom.

Another night, as I sat in my car at the landing watching the necklace of shore lights stringing itself along the Bay from Sandwich to Provincetown, a car with four teenagers in it pulled up beside me, one couple in front, the other in back. I saw their young faces in the blue glare of their Bics as they lit up cigarettes. They remain parked there for nearly an hour, the radio softly humming, the windows gradually clouding up. Every ten minutes or so, the one in the driver's seat would get out and slip into the backseat, while another would get out of the back on the other side and go to the front. I watched, fascinated, as this round-robin makeout continued, punctuated now and then by brief butane flares, until, all permutations and participants apparently exhausted, the last one in the driver's seat drove them all away.

The landing, I think, also adds to the social character of the town, serving as trysting place, outdoor office, and conference room, or simply as a topic of conversation itself. Walking along the beach there, I have heard the conversations of local or vacationing businessmen, discussing prospects and promotions, carried in the wind. Sometimes I meet the local officials—planning-board or finance-committee members—engaged in what one of them likes to call "shellfish diplomacy."

One day last April, following a freak late-winter blizzard, I met Charlie Ellis coming out of the small market at the other end of Paine's Creek Road. We spent a few minutes discussing changes wrought by the storm at the landing—alterations of its creek banks, erosion of its dunes, shifts in the sandbars offshore. Holding our bags of groceries, we speculated on its history and its future, no less complex and uncertain than our own.

Thus there is still a kind of natural and local sociability in this town that would most likely have been gone by now in inland communities as far down the development road as we are. Though the land has lost much, if not most, of its open, rural character, the sea still presses in upon us as a living presence near such meeting places. Ironically, it is the very narrowness of our land that forces a wide outlook upon us and still saves us to some degree.

4

The town landing is a good place from which to begin any season, but early spring is the time of year when I like to drive down to see what the winter has left us to start over with. The gulls already know, lined up along the marsh banks of the creek, waiting patiently for the arrival of the alewives. But for me the directives are not so clear, and new assessments are in order.

"Early spring," in this land where the cold ocean retards and sometimes even obliterates the season, can mean anytime up to the first of June. Still, though it is only mid-April, several cars are already sprawled in the parking lot when I arrive at the landing. The day began gray, damp, and leaden, but now, at noon, the cloud cover has shredded apart and the sun, as high as it will be in August, beats down on waters still too cold for wading.

Most of the people seem content to stay in their cars, soaking up the spring sun without the raw wind that accompanies it. Parked next to me, a man in a yellow Pinto has fallen asleep, his head thrown back on the seat, snoring loudly through the open window. A police cruiser drives up and, apparently spotting no violations or disturbances among the periwinkles, lingers several minutes before driving off again. Behind me, a little ways up the creek, a young man wearing a red mackinaw is setting minnow traps. His female companion slips in the swift currents, landing with a loud, wet slap on her bottom. He turns and barks at her, "Dumb broad, if you're gonna cross a river you don't stop!"

Loud rock music blares from a low-slung, custom-painted Trans-Am, carrying far out over the flats. It grates as a raw intrusion in a place that needs no human enhancement or accompaniment. How ironic, I think, that the world has such a need to come to places like this, yet insists on dragging with it so much of what it wants to leave behind. We seem to have lost the knack of looking at anything now without bracketing it in some kind of artificial frame or manufactured noise, and our technology more often serves as a means of keeping the environment at arm's or wheel's length than as a means of extending ourselves into it. And yet, who am I to criticize, who for all the time I've spent here have yet to learn to walk naked on this beach?

So I get out of the car and begin to walk north, down over the rock riprap fronting the parking lot, across the narrow beach, through the thin border of marsh grass, and once more out onto the open flats. Not that long ago, it seems, these same flats were littered at low tide with great blocks of salt ice higher than a man's head, stranded mammoths doomed to extinction. Now nothing of their recent, dominating presence remains. The sands have been swept clean of winter, and everywhere the signs of a new season can be seen. Crows flap like shiny shadows across the marsh stubble where periwinkles, their snail shells dried pale by the sun and wind, huddle among the stalks. A yellowlegs pokes and bobs along the peat ledges bordering the beach. Back in the low dunes, among the sharp-tipped bouquets of new beach-grass sprouts, I hear the thin trilling of a savannah sparrow rippling on the wind.

I walk farther out, following the wide, shallow course of Paine's Creek as it winds its way over the flats. Its shining, shaking waters are planted with gulls, like small trees. A few winter brant linger in the shallows, feeding on eelgrass. The whole, disparate scene is held together by a wide web of veined waters, lilting outward, braiding and unbraiding in their common flow toward the oncoming tide. Once again the beauty of unity, of life and all its elements held in such wide, unfettered play, sweeps away any need for questions about meaning. All the shifting components of fluid motion and easy grace seem now to hold no intimations of revelation, no teasing suggestions or hidden analogies. This is ultimate, overt statement of the clearest and most complete kind, letting me know that any spot is a port of entry if we will only accept it for what it is, asking of me only that I bear witness and recognize myself for what I so manifestly am: a part of what I behold.

As I go out, the flats give the illusion of rising slightly before me in alternating layers of exposed bars and blue channels. The waters beyond spread out to the mirage line of the horizon, where, to the northeast, whole sections of bluffs in Truro and Wellfleet hang like floating islands over the Bay with a line of blue sky drawn beneath them. Finally the stream channel swings sharply east, blocking my further progress. On the bars beyond the channel, the sands are dotted with the white, exposed shells of sea clams, but the channel waters are too deep and swift and cold. I will go out for them another time.

I turn and look back toward the landing. The number of cars in the parking lot has grown; they line up in ranks now, facing the Bay, like racers at a starting line or rockets on a launchpad. The people are beginning to spill down onto the beach and out onto the flats. Beyond them the land begins its gentle rise into the dark folds of the morainal ridge where, somewhere, my house lies hidden. Beyond the land great banks of sculptured white cumulus clouds rise tier upon rounded tier, like dream mountains. The clouds, a product of warm-air thermals rising from the heated land and cooling above it, form a suspended river running down the length of the Cape and tracing its shape. Beginning far to the west, where the canal power plant lifts its massive stack to the sky, they roll down the low hills of the upper Cape, flatten and thin as they round the elbow at Orleans, become fleecy washes of white as they drift north down the tilted plains of the outer Cape, and finally disappear completely as they near the pencil-thin spire of the Pilgrim Monument at Provincetown.

I begin walking back in toward the landing, passing as I do

several people whom I know coming out: a neighbor with her two small children, a postal clerk, the school librarian. Their tracks, large and small, shod and unshod, mix in the wet sand with those of the gulls, with the grooved, winding trails of moon snails and the corded patterns left by the receding wavelets of the last tide.

Unlike the fish and the birds, we have no clear, unambiguous directions to our lives. Yet spring still asks extensions of us, pushing up from under the accumulated debris and the storms of winter, a new re-entry into life. On these flats, etched with so many different marks, I trace the hieroglyphs of our own need for participation: here a clam rake was dragged; here someone's lazy saunter broke out into wide leaps of enthusiasm; here a tentative hole was dug.

On the beach a young girl is leading her chestnut mare down onto the flats and out across the bright running streams. The horse kicks and starts, excited at the sudden space and openness. She wants to run, but the girl holds her in check, forcing her to walk with controlled passion in a wide circle out from the beach. Her long, black hair and the animal's dark mane blow back together in the wind. Behind them the broad, sweeping arm of the Cape curves round to the east, swinging north and peeling down to nothing on the horizon, gathering us all in.

Afterword

Anyone who writes about the current scene on Cape Cod is lucky if major changes or developments in his material do not occur before it is printed. I am happy, however, to report one change that has taken place since this book was written. In 1980 the Town of Brewster bought for conservation the land on which the old Black homestead stood. The house was given to the Brewster Historical Society, carefully dismantled, and reconstructed by John MacKenzie, a local builder, next to the society's 1790 windmill on Route 6A in West Brewster.

—R.F.